Russian Voices on the Kennebec:
The Story of Maine's Unlikely Colony

RUSSIAN VOICES ON THE KENNEBEC

THE STORY OF MAINE'S UNLIKELY COLONY

by Robert S. Jaster

THE UNIVERSITY OF MAINE PRESS

ORONO, MAINE 1999

06 05 04 03 02 01 00 99   1 2 3 4 5

ISBN: 0-89101-097-1

The paper used in this publication meets the minimum requirements of the American National Standard for Information Sciences—Permanence of Paper for Printed Library Materials, ansi z39.48-1984. Printed and bound in the United States of America. Book design by Michael Alpert.

Photograph on front cover: Alexandra Sherbakoff as a Georgian folkdancer, 1930s. Courtesy of Alexandra Sherbakoff. *Photographs on back cover (top), from left to right:* (1) Russian farmer Boris Dulkin and his animals, early 1960s. Photograph by Freeda Witham. (2) Anna Wdowin, and Tamara Wdowin, "mermaids" in production of "Golden Lake," a Russian fairytale, 1959. Photograph by Freeda Witham. (3) Artist Nikodin Belenkov painting icons in St. Alexander Nevsky Church, 1950s. Photograph by Freeda Witham.

CONTENTS

A GALLERY OF PHOTOGRAPHS CAN BE FOUND AFTER PAGE 52

INTRODUCTION

THE KENNEBEC VALLEY IN 1950 SLEPT QUIETLY in the shadow of its thriving and industrious past. Its wide river, flanked by rolling farmland and forest, gave the area a calm, pastoral beauty. But it was also an area of stagnant agriculture, little industry, and declining population. Richmond—the largest town between the shipbuilding center of Bath forty miles to the south and the state capital of Augusta about fifteen miles north—had a population of 1,600, half that of its heyday in the 1890s. Many local family names, mainly of British origin, but some with German, French, or Scandinavian roots, had appeared on town tax-rolls for generations. Foreign accents had long since become a rarity along the Kennebec.

By any measure the valley seemed an unlikely place to plant a colony of Russian-speaking refugees. Job prospects were bleak, and urban amenities few. Nor was there a local Russian enclave to welcome any new arrivals with the traditional bread and salt. Yet they came: Great Russians, Ukrainians, Belorussians, and Cossacks; professors, peasants and farmers, artists, and carpenters. Many came directly from Europe's Displaced Persons camps, where they had landed following the massive diaspora of people fleeing the U.S.S.R. toward the end of World War II. Others came from cities across America where they had settled earlier—some in the early 1920s, after fleeing the Russian revolution and civil war (1917-22). They all shared a common language, their Orthodox faith, a zest for life, and a hatred of the Soviet regime. By the end of the 1950s several hundred of these Russian-speaking families, representing all the ethnic groups mentioned above, had settled among the valley's towns and countryside. Richmond had become the center of a unique colony: the largest rural Russian-speaking settlement in America. Soon Richmond had a Russian restaurant, a Russian boot-maker's shop, and the onion-shaped dome of St. Alexander Nevsky, Maine's first Russian Orthodox church rose at the top of Church Street. For the first time Russian was heard on the streets of Richmond, Dresden, Pittston, Bowdoinham and the other small towns strung along the valley. Russian-speaking children were enrolling in the local schools.

To local "Mainers" the ethnic distinctions between Great Russians, Belorussians, Ukrainians, and Cossacks proved too confusing, so all the settlers were referred to as "Russians"—a generic label which the settlers themselves came to use in speaking of their fellow colonists. In this book the same usage has been adopted: "Russians" refers to *all* the Russian-speaking settlers, not only those of Great Russian nationality.

This book is the first to be written about life in this historically unique community. Who were these settlers? Why did they choose to congregate in Maine's Kennebec Valley? How did they live their lives—personal, social, spiritual, and political—in the colony? Where did they find work? How did they interact with the local Mainers?

The core of the book is a group of individuals' stories, told mainly in their own words and based on extensive personal interviews conducted in English and Russian over a three-year period, 1994-96. They were selected because of their intrinsic interest, personal and historical, and because they represent a broad spectrum of the colonists and their offspring. These stories are arranged roughly by generation: Part One, the so-called "Old Émigrés" of the *Pervaya Volna* (First Wave) who fled Russia around 1917-21—that is, before the Bolsheviks had come to power and reconstituted it as the Soviet Union; Part Two, the *Vtoraya Volna* (Second Wave), who left the U.S.S.R., most as refugees, during the last months of World War II; and Part Three, their Russian-American children, born outside the U.S.S.R. in the early postwar years.

The first two chapters explore the origins of the settlement. Chapter One tells the story of Baron Vladimir von Poushental, the colony's swashbuckling founder. That venture, inspired by both altruism and financial need, enabled hundreds of Russian Orthodox immigrants to find "a place to drop their anchor," as he once put it, in a spiritually congenial harbor. His profits from the venture enabled him to live as a local bon vivant, and perhaps helped him toward his greatest social success: marriage to a wealthy American widow. Chapter Two recounts the previously untold story of the *Russkii Corpus*—the White Russian Corps—and its pivotal role in settling the colony and exerting strong direction over its early religious and political activities.

To give context to the personal stories that follow Chapter Two, background material was drawn from Russian-language sources, local press files, town and county records, and interviews with non-Russian residents in the valley, as well as various published materials on Church history and the final months of World War II in Central Europe. Part Four offers a narrative assessment and summary of the life of the colony—the main events, concerns, activities, and relationships of the settlers over a forty-year span. This book thus fills in a vital and colorful missing chapter in America's immigrant history in the post-World War II period.

PART ONE

FIRST WAVE: THE OLD ÉMIGRÉS (1917–1922)

There are many of us "old Russians" who didn't choose Richmond, Maine, like "elephants coming together in the last to die." We came here to live and to build. Some of us lost hundreds of acres of land, estates and mansions, converted to museums after the Revolution in Russia. In Europe we toiled, saved, built and lost again. Now, in the fifties, we considered ourselves fortunate to become part of this country. This time we were ready to build again, true . . . on a smaller scale, with less strength. . . . but that does not stop us from living life, tending our gardens and wanting to be useful.

–Anna Tuniks, letter to *Kennebec Journal*, May 11, 1968

—9—

CHAPTER ONE

FOUNDER OF THE COLONY:
THE MYSTERIOUS WHITE BARON

IT WAS THE AUTUMN OF 1948, AND LARRY CHADWICK JR.,
a local teenager, was hunting alone on a quiet stretch of the East
River, a fork of the Kennebec, where he had placed some old decoys.
"I was watching a flock of ducks, and had some luck knocking them
out of the sky. And suddenly, on the other bank of the river this man
stands up and comes out from behind the trees, shouting to me. He'd
evidently been watching me for some time. 'Should I send my dog
to go after the birds?', he asks. I'd seen him once or twice in the village, and knew he was this Russian guy who people said had moved
up here. I told him no, that wasn't necessary, as I had hip-boots on.
Then he complimented me on the way the decoys were set out, and
on my shooting. So of course I was pleased. Next time we met he
invited me to go hunting with him."

At that time few local people knew Vladimir von Poushental, or
what he was doing in Maine. He had bought up a few distressed
farms, and in 1949 he opened a one-man real estate office in the village of Gardiner. But it seemed to be a low-key, part-time business.
Local people were of course unaware of the advertisements he had
begun to place in Russian-language newspapers throughout the
United States. Typical was the one appearing in *Novoye Russkoye
Slovo (The New Russian Word)*, New York, of 1 May 1950:

РУССКИЕ! ШТАТ МЭЙН ЖДЕТ ВАС!
ОТЛИЧНАЯ ОХОТА И РЫБНАЯ ЛОВЛЯ,
ПРЕКРАСНЫЙ КЛИМАТ.
ПО СЛУЧАЮ ПРОДАЕТСЯ ДОМ:
8 комнат, гараж, подвал, 30 акров земли, яблочный сад
за 2.500 долларов.
Там же земля недалеко от реки — 20 дол. за акр.
Звонить по вечерам по телефону: PL. 3—2285
или писать по адресу:
Miss Cosgrove, R 4, Gardiner, Maine.

RUSSIANS! THE STATE OF MAINE AWAITS YOU!
Excellent Hunting and Fishing, a Beautiful Climate. House for Sale:
8 rooms, garage, cellar, 30 acres, apple orchard, $2,500. . . .

Poushental seems too flamboyant and adventurous a character to
have settled for so humdrum an activity as flogging run-down properties in the Kennebec Valley, particularly in the decade following
World War II, when it was an area of severe economic blight and few
social or cultural attractions. The Poushental family had been
wealthy landowners in Austria-Hungary until the early 1800s, when
Vladimir's great-grandfather was discovered engaging in clandestine
political activities on behalf of the Russian government. Forced to
flee the ancestral estate, he was rewarded by the Tsar with a title and
extensive landholdings in Russia. With the Tsar's patronage, the
Poushentals soon regained the wealth and social status they had
enjoyed before.

Vladimir was born in 1894 to Princess Angelicoss of the Greek
royal family and Baron Kuhn von Poushental, a general in the
Russian engineering corps. Young Poushental attended military
academy before joining the Tsar's army as a captain in 1915. At age
twenty-one he became one of Imperial Russia's first combat pilots.
Later he recalled his first solo flight. Since the trainer craft were sin-
gle-seaters, flight instructors could not go into the air with their students. "[One day] I made a couple of turns on the landing-field . . .
I thought 'I will try to fly.' When I came down again I said, 'It's *terrible!*' . . . They said, '*That* plane is not for flying. It's just for taxiing
around the airfield.'" The plane he later flew in combat for Russia's

Black Sea squadron had no machine guns or other mounted weapons. Poushental carried a pistol and a cockpit full of bombs, which he dropped by hand on enemy docks in Constantinople. He was eventually shot down over the Black Sea, but managed to stay afloat until a Russian cruiser picked him up.[1]

When Russia's civil war erupted, Poushental joined General Wrangel's White Army in the Crimea.* After Red Army forces broke through Wrangel's lines in November 1920, the General disbanded his troops. He told them they could either remain in Russia or report to ships in Sevastopol to be taken to sanctuary abroad. "I went to the Sevastopol Harbor with a friend. We were stopped five or six blocks from the pier and told to leave the car and to take with us whatever we could carry in our two hands. I left Russia with a couple of suitcases." One held 25 million rubles in Tsarist notes—the last of the Poushental family fortune, then worth 12.5 million United States dollars at the official rate of exchange. Russia's currency was falling so fast in the face of Bolshevik victories, however, that Poushental got only $850 for his rubles. Had he waited another day, he said, he would have had to accept $100 less.[2]

Poushental, an expert marksman and a keen hunter, also managed to carry out a favorite hunting rifle. He was evacuated to Turkey, where his fluency in French helped him make contact with members of the local elite. He soon got a job shooting game birds for a dollar each on a vast estate outside Constantinople. "In a couple of days I could shoot a hundred ducks," he said later, "so I made a good living, stayed in a nice hotel, and had fun. But I had always wanted to go to America and play Indians when I was a kid." When the opportunity came to go in 1923, he went. In the United States he looked up George de Bothezat, an old friend of his father's.[3] De Bothezat, a fellow-Russian in spite of the French surname, was an aeronautical engineer and inventive genius who had immigrated to

* The Communist seizure of power in November 1917 led to widespread chaos and civil war in which the nascent Red Army was challenged by volunteer "White"— i.e., anti-Communist—armies formed throughout the fallen Empire. The force led by former Tsarist General Wrangel fell to the Red Army in November 1920. A few White forces held out a year or two longer but, by 1922, when the U.S.S.R. was officially founded, the Communist regime had taken control over all but a few pockets of the dead Tsar's realm.

the United States several years earlier to design a helicopter for the United States Army Air Service. His craft was powered by rotors mounted at the ends of four long struts, giving it the appearance of something bolted together from a giant erector set. But in February 1922, de Bothezat's "Flying Octopus" stayed aloft for one minute forty-two seconds, becoming the first helicopter to achieve actual flight. The Army soon lost interest, however, and canceled the project.[4]

In 1925 de Bothezat organized a private firm to manufacture coaxial helicopters and industrial blowers. Poushental became his personal assistant, and later general manager of the Helicopter Corporation of America. The company prospered until 1940, when de Bothezat died suddenly and, as Poushental laconically explained afterward, "took his secrets with him." There had been other problems as well. The Corporation's chief engineer later wrote of financial difficulties and the new management's "disregard of [de Bothezat's] theories. Slowly, in spite of the efforts of a very few associates, the organization faded out of the picture."[5] By the mid-1940s Poushental, who had thought he was on the way to becoming a millionaire in the helicopter business, found himself without a job.

By then he had experienced too many unexpected turns of fortune to be deeply troubled by this latest setback. He once told a friend, somewhat disingenuously, "I came into this world with nothing, and I expect to leave the same way." Larry Chadwick Jr., his hunting companion, later said that Poushental "was a man who lived an exquisite life before the downfall of the Tsar, but he didn't dwell on it. If it was Beluga caviar one day and baloney the next, it didn't make one bit of difference to him."[6] He had learned to swim with the current, which occasionally beached him on an inhospitable bank; but he had also learned to reach out and grasp whatever opportunity came along to rescue himself.

His greatest opportunity eventually came in Maine. Poushental first visited the state on a hunting trip with an old wartime friend, Simon de Korsakoff, ex-commander of the Tsar's Black Sea air squadron and great nephew of the composer, Nikolai Rimsky-Korsakoff. The pair stayed in Boothbay Harbor, from which they explored the largely uninhabited woods along the Kennebec River in their search for game.[7] Following the collapse of the Helicopter Corporation, Poushental left New York and began living quietly in the back country of the Kennebec Valley, close to the streams and fields and woods which he had roamed with rifle and fishing rod on past vacations. Pittston, the closest village, was little more than a sleepy crossroads that had seen better days since its founding in colonial times. Larry Chadwick recalls that Poushental's house was "a little old cape back in the woods. It had so many stuffed animals and skins, including a stuffed tiger skin, you could hardly get around. And in those days he drove around the countryside in an old station wagon."

Chadwick, a Maine guide who came to know Poushental well at that time, recalls his friend's skills and enjoyment in the field. "He loved to hunt with a good dog. And he was such a good shot. I've seen him shoot grouse on the wing with a 300 Savage, and he'd call the shot beforehand. Once he shot a fox so far away you could just barely see it. He could hit a deer so easily . . . he always said a deer was such a big target. And there was never a safety problem with him . . . you never had to look around to see if a gun was pointed at the calf of your leg."

Freeda Witham, a local journalist who knew Poushental, recalls the time his shooting led to trouble with the state game authorities. "He was on the riverbank with a group one day—it was the hunting season, all right. He had his rifle, and a flock of geese flew overhead. Somebody said 'I bet you can't hit one with that rifle.' He said, 'I bet I can.' Then he brought one of those geese down. And I'll be damned if they didn't put it in the local newspaper, and the next day the Game Warden picked him up, and he got arrested and fined! You can only use birdshot on birds, you know; it's illegal to shoot them with a rifle. But he laughed off the whole affair, and was quite proud of it . . . told me, 'That was quite a trick, you know?'"

Frequently Poushental's hunting and fishing companions included one or two close local friends, particularly Louis Torrey Tasso, an exile from the Central European aristocracy. Such occasions would often be followed by a supper of fish or game at the Chadwicks' home. "When they got together they would laugh and drink and tell stories. There would usually be four or five of us but sometimes as many as eighty . . . all very informal . . . our neighbors would come over . . . Poushental liked everybody. He would sing songs sometimes, but only when he was drunk; and he would tell the bawdiest tales of when he was in the Russian air corps. He was quick to smile and laugh. Everything seemed to please him."

Press photos of Poushental in his early sixties show a trimly dressed man who apparently favored sports jackets, white shirts, and colorful bow ties or a carved turquoise bola. He is friendly-looking, by no means handsome. The dark, thinning hair is combed straight back from a high and rounded forehead. His prominent nose, flaring to a ski-jump at its tip, would not quite pass for Cyrano's. The wide mouth is caught open in an amiable half-smile, as though the shutter had clicked as he was approaching the punch-line of a favorite story.

Unlike some of his hunting friends, Poushental liked to rough it, says Chadwick. "He was a rugged guy, not awfully tall, not six feet. But he had big, heavy hands, and must have been terribly strong when he was young. And he was not a fancy dresser when he hunted. He wore an old-fashioned Woolwich jacket and green wool pants that wouldn't make any noise . . . he bought those at Fred Handley's general store. He'd tuck them into Wellington boots. He was given to wearing a Tyrolean hat. That was his only distinguishing piece of clothing.

"When I took Louis Torrey Tasso fishing he'd bring along some exotic cheeses, smoked meats, and a bottle of vintage wine. It was like going on a gourmet picnic. But when I took Mr. Poushental out, he would stop at a store and we'd buy some bananas and baloney and a loaf of bread and a bottle of ordinary wine, and throw it all in a bag on the front seat of the car. He always liked eating out in the woods. Sometimes I'd cook a meal there—he liked a cooked meal. And he was amazed that anyone could do a whole meal in a big cast-iron skillet."

But Poushental, while continuing to enjoy these pleasures of rustication, also saw an opportunity to make money in Maine real estate. Since the Kennebec Valley was a truly depressed area at that time, few people shared his optimistic assessment. By the late 1940s two-thirds of its small dairy farms had been abandoned as their owners lacked the financial resources to meet the dairies' growing demands for large-scale bulk deliveries.[8] Other rural families had moved to Portland or Bath during World War II to take advantage of high-wage jobs in shipbuilding and other employment opened up during the war. Loggers, too, contributed to the property glut by offering cut-over timber land for as little as a dollar an acre to avoid paying further taxes on it.[9] In 1948 Poushental had begun buying abandoned rural properties on a modest scale, starting with seven small farms in the Pittston area. He established his own real estate firm, Kennebec Realty, the following year. It was capitalized at $60,000.[10] "Poushental would buy a farm with, say, forty acres," says a local acquaintance who had declined Poushental's offer to join his real estate venture, "then later he would sell the house and twenty acres. So in a few years he acquired a lot of land that way."[11] He also had been placing classified advertisements in Russian-language newspapers around the United States extolling the attractions of the Maine countryside ("The climate and land are like Russia's," one read), as well as the low cost of properties, and Maine's congenial lifestyle.[12]

In placing such advertisements, Poushental, who had maintained ties to the White Russian community in America, was aware that many thousands of Russian-speaking refugees were among the waves of Displaced Persons arriving in this country from Europe in the immediate post-World War II period. Between 1947 and 1951 more than 130,000 Russian-speaking Displaced Persons immigrated to the United States.[13] They included "First Wave" refugees—people who had left Russia before the Communist takeover and had settled elsewhere in Europe—as well as "Second Wave" refugees: those who had lived in the Soviet Union until the War had uprooted them. Large numbers of the new arrivals settled first around New York and the industrial towns of New Jersey, where they found jobs and where most lived in predominantly Slavic neighborhoods.

But Poushental's vision went far beyond the sale of scattered run-down farms to these people. His self-proclaimed goal was to establish a White Russian colony, centered in the Kennebec Valley town of Richmond. There the survivors and families of those who had served the White Russian cause could live out their lives in peace among others who spoke their language and who shared their cultural background and Orthodox faith, as well as their hostility toward Communism.

Poushental saw the chance to realize his vision in the spring of 1952, when a thousand veterans of the *Russkii Corpus*, the White Russian Corps, together with their families, arrived in the United States as refugees.[14] The *Corpus* was made up of Russian émigrés who had been living quietly in Yugoslavia until World War II, when they were organized into a military force under the Germans. Poushental seems to have felt a special kinship with these aging warriors who, like him, had fought against the Bolsheviks in Russia's civil war and had fled into exile in 1920. In 1941 they had taken up arms again in the futile hope that the Germans would help them liberate their homeland from Stalinist rule. "These were brave men and women," Poushental said later. "When I read of the arrival of some of the White Corps survivors in the United States, I felt that they should not be forgotten. They had fought on as long as they could. I thought it was the psychological moment to let them know that their lost cause was appreciated."[15]

Shortly after the *Corpus* arrived, Poushental went to New York City to meet its commandant, Colonel Anatoli Rogozhin. "I told him 'You *Corpus* members must throw down your anchor somewhere in the U.S.A. I want to introduce you to Maine, and perhaps you will like it there.' So he and his aide came with me, and I showed them Richmond, and a farm of 300 acres with good fields, a river, and creeks. Colonel Rogozhin told me it was a good place, but they had no money to buy it. I said I didn't want money; I wanted to donate it as a gift to the *Corpus*. Then I went to the Governor of Maine and told him I wanted to organize a White Russian colony of people who had fought against the Bolsheviks. I said, 'I want your blessing . . . and remember, they are White Russians, not Communists.'"[16]

In May 1952 Poushental introduced Colonel Rogozhin to Governor Frederick G. Payne, who welcomed the *Corpus* to Maine. At a press conference in the state capitol Rogozhin announced his acceptance of Poushental's offer, and outlined his ambitious plans for *Corpus* activities in the new colony. It would, he said, be the world headquarters for the 4,000 surviving *Corpus* veterans, a thousand of whom were now living in the United States. Its leaders would live in Richmond to oversee the farm, he said, using its profits to establish a retirement home for its aging veterans.[17]

With Poushental's assistance the *Corpus* leaders moved quickly to establish its presence in Maine. Three members began living and working on the farm that first summer. In July the St. Alexander Nevsky Foundation was chartered in Maine as the *Corpus'* charitable arm. Named for its patron saint, the foundation was to raise money for its home for the elderly. Poushental was appointed to its board. The Home itself became a reality a few months later with the purchase of a mansion in Richmond. In August 1953 a newly built chapel in the mansion was consecrated as Maine's first Russian Orthodox spiritual center. Thirty-five Russian settlers in the area gathered to meet their "long-awaited pastor."[18]

These events were reported in the local press, and in Russian-language papers, Orthodox Church bulletins, and other media. Well-publicized *Corpus* activities, and particularly the opening of its chapel, acted as a magnet drawing Orthodox Russians, including of course *Corpus* members and their families, to settle in the area. The town of Richmond, which had no Russians on its tax-rolls in 1950, had close to fifty Russian households in 1955 and 130 a decade later. Friends and relatives of recent settlers swelled the ranks of the colony during the summer months. By the 1960s the colony had become the largest rural Russian settlement in the United States. Although the activities and fortunes of the *Corpus'* venture in Maine fell far short of its leaders' original expectations (discussed in chapter 2), Poushental's fortunes flourished. His advertisements in Russian-language papers brought visitors to the area who asked him to show them local properties. By 1954 he owned twenty-five parcels in Richmond township, and another twenty in other parts of the valley. Sales were brisk.

Moreover, as founder and chief benefactor of the White Russian colony, Poushental's public persona blossomed while his real estate venture prospered. Together these successes propelled him rather suddenly from the quiet life of a rural outdoorsman into the cosmopolitan company of wealthy socialites. In 1955 he married Mrs. J. Fred Brown, a widow described by the *Denver Post* as a prominent member of Denver and Philadelphia mainline society who maintained a residence in each city. The wedding took place in the

Chapel of Our Lady of Kursk in New York, Orthodox Bishop Nikon of Florida presiding. A reception at the Park Lane Hotel followed. Later Baron and Baroness von Poushental—in his new milieu he was no longer the unassuming "Vlad" or "Mr. Poushental" known to the folks in Maine—flew to San Francisco to board an oceanliner for a honeymoon trip to Hawaii.[19]

The Poushentals took up residence in Miami, where the Baron entered the local real estate business, and the Baroness became a noted society hostess. The loggia of their home overlooking the Bay frequently made local society columns as the scene of sparkling events. One such was a cocktail party in support of the International Rescue Committee (IRC), a prestigious voluntary agency founded by Albert Einstein to aid refugees worldwide. Among the guests were multimillionaire Angier Biddle Duke, who served as president of the IRC, and Senator Hubert Humphrey who, it was noted, "flew down from Washington and back the next day."[20] Poushental was also a member of the Committee of a Hundred, an influential group of Republican small businessmen.

A number of honorary titles and awards came to the Baron during this period, chiefly in recognition of his work on behalf of the White Russian colony. In 1968 the Knights of Malta, a quasi-religious fraternal organization with spiritual roots going back to the Crusades, bestowed on him the eight-pointed Maltese Cross and the title Knight of Rome in the Order of St. John of Jerusalem. Poushental, who had been a United States citizen since 1930, was made an Honorary Citizen of the United States in 1969, and his achievements entered in the *Congressional Record* by Senator Claude Pepper of Florida.[21]

Poushental continued to spend the summer and fall in Maine, usually staying through the October hunting season. His wife sometimes accompanied him, though only for brief periods. They were easily identified in town by their white, chauffeur-driven Cadillac. In the 1960s he built a picturesque log chalet near Pittston complete with a huge stone fireplace and pine-paneled walls from which the eyes of stuffed moose, elk, deer, and buffalo looked down lugubriously on the Baron and his guests. He named the place Chateau Blue Heron.

Yet Poushental, in spite of his widespread recognition as founder of the White Russian colony, remained a distant figure to the settlers themselves, few of whom seemed to know him well. This was due in part to his aristocratic background. Unlike all but a few of the settlers, Poushental came from the ranks of the lower nobility, spoke upper-class Russian, and had lived in the United States since the 1920s, long enough to have become an accepted participant in mainstream American society. While his knowledge of the language and the "system" of his adoptive country made him invaluable in explaining and interpreting for the newly arrived settlers, it also set him apart from them. The distance further widened with his marriage to a wealthy American woman and his less-frequent appearances in Maine after moving to Miami. Moreover, Poushental seems to have been at heart a truly private person, one who cherished the company of a few close friends and who kept the private side of his life closely guarded. All this, together with stories about his swashbuckling past, of course gave Poushental an aura of mystery and vague danger. Rumors and conjecture were rife among locals and settlers alike. A local friend of his remembers walking into the village store and overhearing talk about a submarine. "Some local people were actually saying that Poushental had somehow put a submarine in Nehumkeag Pond near here—it flows into the Kennebec and is maybe fourteen feet deep at its deepest part—and that he was just waiting for the right moment to launch some sort of attack! People were so paranoid . . . it was the time of the Cold War and the McCarthy hearings. And people around here felt that if you were a Russian, you must be a Communist."

Among the Russian settlers, particularly the women, there were stories and rumors about Poushental's personal life. His sexual involvement with one or two of the colony's younger single women made other women wary and apprehensive about him. Vera Kotov, who was around thirty when she and her husband first settled in Richmond in 1952, recalled walking along the road by herself one day when Poushental drove up beside her and offered her a ride in his Cadillac. "I said 'NO! I'm a married woman!'"[22] Vera had long conversations with one of his girlfriends in the local Turkish bathhouse. "She was a widow who was his mistress as well as his secretary. And when he got married, she cried and told me that she loved him. She was brokenhearted." There were also dark rumors that Poushental had paid off another girlfriend, who may or may not have been pregnant, to leave town shortly before his marriage.[23] But if some of the women felt Poushental to be sexually threatening, others saw him as a somewhat comic Don Juan whose romantic entanglements were not to be taken too seriously. Two former acquaintances, neither of whom were ever romantically involved with Poushental, described him as a *shlyapa*, Russian for "hat," but also a slang word for a man who is impractical and a little slow to catch on. Nor did he strike Alexandra Sherbakoff as the smooth, seductive type. "He always reminded me of a bull," she says. "It was hard to believe that he was once a *dvoryanin* [wealthy landowner]."[24]

A far more romantic Poushental emerges from the recollections of Larry Chadwick Jr., youngest of a handful of Poushental's friends who were his close companions on many hunting, fishing, and informal social occasions during his years in Maine. Few people—probably none now living—knew the private Poushental better than Chadwick. "He was an outstanding ladies' man," says Chadwick. "*Outstanding*. He could have outdone Cyrano de Bergerac in a second, such a swordsman was he. It was great to be around someone who exuded good manners, no harsh language . . . a gentleman with a twinkle in his eye. He never said or did anything that would be offensive to a woman present. And he would always pick flowers for all the ladies."

The Russian settlers were also divided, or at best ambivalent, about other aspects of Poushental's character and personality. Some whispered that he was a Muslim—a thoroughly discredited notion— who should be denied the sacraments of the Orthodox church. Others simply found him aloof and snobbish. Yet Vera Kotov recalled the time Poushental noticed a family standing among their belongings outside the house which he had sold them a few years before. "They had been evicted . . . had lost their jobs, couldn't pay the mortgage. He put them in his Cadillac and took them to stay in his own house."

His real estate dealings, too, received mixed reviews from the Russian settlers. The anecdotal record suggests that Poushental showed a casual, somewhat unprofessional attitude toward his business. Pavel Vaulin, who had previously bought one or two rural properties in Richmond, went out with Poushental one day to look for another. "We walked through the woods to see land he had for sale along the river. When we got there he said, 'Well, Pavel, what do you think of it?' I said, 'It's fine. In fact, I already own it'. He was trying to sell me my own land!"[25] More than one settler, however, bought a farm from Poushental which a later survey showed to be substantially larger than that specified in the purchase contract. Even the "300-acre farm" he gave to the White Russian *Corpus* turned out to contain 400 acres. Yet one settler, offered a farm for $4,000 by Poushental, was able to buy it from its actual owner for $1,800.[26] Whatever the explanation, purchase at the higher price would have profited Poushental as broker at the expense of his fellow-immigrant.

Freeda Witham, a retired reporter who covered the Russian colony's activities for the local press, says that the settlers "were well aware that he was pretty sharp, see. But the point was, he *was* the means of their getting this property, and they *knew* it. Most of them knew he wasn't losing any money on it. So there were those amongst them who would give you the impression 'It's very nice that he's given us this opportunity; if it wasn't for him we wouldn't have been able to do this. But we'll watch him all the same!'"[27]

By the early 1970s Poushental and his wife had separated. Although he continued to spend half the year in Miami, he returned to Chateau Blue Heron more often and for longer periods after that. "I'd take him sculling on the Kennebec hunting for duck," Larry Chadwick says of this period, "but he had quit hunting with dogs. He seemed like an ageless guy, but I noticed he had gotten a little slower." By then Poushental was in his seventies.

Poushental died in Miami in December 1978 at the age of 84. His will provided bequests totaling $25,000, including $5,000 for the St. Alexander Nevsky Church and like amounts for another Orthodox church, an Orthodox Bishop, and three women friends. Alas, the bequests could not be carried out: Poushental's total assets came to only $22,000—less than the total bequests—and the will itself was challenged by his estranged wife. His wish to be buried in the small hillside cemetery in Dresden, Maine *was* carried out, however. His gravestone bears two engravings: an Orthodox cross, and the figures of a hunter and his dog. Larry Chadwick remembers that only five or six people—Poushental's lawyer and a few friends—came to the funeral. Poushental could look back on many achievements in his long and adventurous life, including those of fighter pilot, corporate manager, sportsman, and prominent socialite. Yet he told friends that he was proudest of his initiative in founding the colony for White Russian refugees. In his later years he spoke affectionately of these peoples' successful transplant, of settlers with their chicken farms and beehives who had transformed their new environment into something close to "the Russia that used to be," he said. "So we have . . . the Russian shoemaker, the Russian restaurant, the Russian playhouse. People come from New York to the Russian bakery and buy the Russian caviar. There are three churches, two Russian and one Ukrainian." Except for the touch of it in Maine, he said in 1968, "there is no land of Russia in all the world. Russia does not exist any more. . . . There is no such country."[28]

The Russian restaurant and bakery and shoemaker's shop are gone now, along with their owners. Among the area's Russian-speaking residents today only a handful of the oldest settlers remember Poushental at all.

CHAPTER TWO

RUSSKII CORPUS COMES TO TOWN:
A NEW LIFE FOR OLD WARRIORS

FEW TIES ARE STRONGER OR MORE ENDURING than the bond among men who have fought side by side in battle. If proof were needed, we have only to look at the annual reunions still being held by various United States military units that fought in World War II, more than fifty years in our past. Imagine, then, how much stronger such bonds would be if, say, the United States Seventh Cavalry were made up of fathers who had served together in the First and Second World Wars and their sons who joined them in fighting the Second.

It is this two-generational family bonding which distinguishes the *Russkii Corpus* from virtually any other existing military unit, and which largely accounts for the enduring close ties among its members. The fathers fought in the Tsar's army in World War I and served together in the White forces in Russia's civil war which immediately followed. The 1920s and 1930s saw 75,000 of these Russian veterans and their families reestablish their Russian lifestyles and distinctive Russian culture in their self-imposed exile in Yugoslavia.

The institutions they created there included a special Russian high school to train their sons as officers who they hoped would one day return to Russia, leading an army of liberation. The first cohorts of these Cadets, who were born in the early 1920s, graduated around

1940-41, just as the Second World War was about to engulf Yugoslavia.

The leaders of its White Russian community saw Germany's invasion of the U.S.S.R. in June 1941 as an opportunity to take a leading role in the long-hoped-for liberation of their homeland. Gennadi Sisoyan, a *Corpus* historian writing in 1952, described the unit's origins.[1] Spokesman for the community's war veterans was the former Tsarist General Skorodumov, "who dreamed of resuming the struggle against the Bolsheviks. . . . Believing Hitler's promises to establish an independent Russia, he asked the German authorities permission to form a Russian Corps . . . The Germans agreed, and in November 1941 the formation of the *Corpus* began." The 400 Cadets made up a special battalion. The *Corpus* wore German *Wehrmacht* uniforms, but with a distinctive red, white, and blue shoulder-patch.

By then the bonds among the old veterans had been strengthened by intermarriage among the next generation. Typical of this group is Lydia Rostov (not her real name; she insisted on anonymity). Born in Belgrade in 1926 and graduated from the Russian gymnasium there, she married a Cadet at the outbreak of war in Yugoslavia. "I came from a military family, and I seem to get along particularly well with military people," she said. "My father was an officer in the Tsar's army who joined the Whites in the civil war. My husband was a Cadet who joined the *Corpus* the year it was organized." While some *Corpus* members, particularly among the older, more senior officers, were motivated to join by strong patriotic convictions, some joined the 10,000-man unit for other reasons. "It was established on a 'voluntary-compulsory' basis," writes Sisoyan, explaining that this meant "some joined its ranks in order to provide food for their families, while others were forced to sign up or be deprived of work."[2]

The mission assigned the new force by the German High Command, however, was not at all what *Corpus* leaders and recruits had been led to expect. "The dreams of the General to fight against the Bolsheviks were not realized," says Sisoyan with dry understatement. Instead of being sent to the Eastern Front, the *Corpus* was split up and ordered to defend power plants, railways, mines and other strategic points in Yugoslavia against attack by Tito's guerrillas. In 1944, when Yugoslav partisans stepped up their guerrilla war against the German occupation, the *Corpus* was assigned to wage a counter-offensive against them. Major Cherepov, second-in-command of the *Corpus*, later reminded fellow *"Corpusniks"* of their sacrifices in that bloody campaign:

> Scattered by Company and Battalion all across Serbia, our *Corpus* . . . endured great hardships. We remember (the battles) of Zvornik, Khomolye, Biely Kamen, the valley of the Ibro. All this is still fresh in our memories. Hundreds of graves mark the places where we served and fought hard battles, including the thousand-kilometer winter march through Bosnia's mountains.[3]

As Soviet forces closed in on the Balkans in the final weeks of the war, the *Corpus* fought its way through partisan-controlled territory to escape to Austria. There the *Corpus* surrendered weapons to British troops, and its members were interned in a British-run camp near St. Veit. Over the next six years (1945-51) their fate remained in doubt as Stalin demanded that, under the terms of the Yalta accord, they be handed over to Soviet forces to be taken to the U.S.S.R.* Since they had served under German command, they would have faced certain execution by the Soviets.

A former *Corpus* member later described the fears and gnawing uncertainties of those years. "Our future was completely uncertain and unknown. Nerves were stretched to the limits. No one knew what to expect. Some members of the staff and some private soldiers gradually scattered, seeking their families. We remember the visit of an international commission, including Soviet military, to our camp,

---

* The Yalta agreements were signed by Stalin, Roosevelt, and Churchill in the Soviet Black Sea port of Yalta in February 1945. These far-reaching accords set forth a blueprint for the postwar world order, as well as an agenda for Allied cooperation in the final months of the war. Sub-agreements between the Western and Soviet military commands dealt with the thorny issue of repatriating millions of refugees and displaced persons, as well as Allied prisoners of war. The paragraph that was to cause much discord and great human suffering provided that all Soviet citizens liberated by American and British forces would be kept in camps until handed over to Soviet military authorities for return to the U.S.S.R. Toward the end of 1945, however, news of the brutality and injustice of this forcible repatriation led American officials to limit repatriation to Soviet soldiers and known collaborators with the Germans (*see* chapter five, "A Cossack Interlude").

and our fears when that was followed by the arrest of our Commandant, Colonel Rogozhin, who was taken away; and our relief when he was brought back that night."[4] The same *Corpus* veteran noted the crucial role played by Colonel Rogozhin in sustaining *Corpus* morale and discipline in the camp. "On his orders various courses were taught: for example, construction, auto repair, and English, so that we would not become despondent. He had a chapel and theater built in the woods. Colonel Rogozhin also approached officials of the Allied High Command to make them aware of who these people were who belonged to the *Corpus*, and of their long-standing armed struggle against Communism." Rogozhin's initiative eventually convinced the Western Allies that *Corpus* members had never been Soviet citizens, and therefore were exempt from forcible "repatriation" to the Soviet Union under the Yalta agreement. His diplomatic success made it possible for the United States to grant the *Corpus* and *Corpus* families special permission to emigrate to the United States—the only foreign military unit to have served under German command in World War II to be given what was, in effect, a blanket amnesty for having done so.

Such was the background of the thousand-odd *Corpus* members and their families who arrived in New York City in the early spring of 1952 to be met by Baron von Poushental with an offer of free land in Richmond, Maine. The healthy and more active members quickly set about seeking jobs and places to live, mainly in the cities and towns of eastern New York and New Jersey. Colonel Rogozhin chartered the *Corpus* in New York state as the Union of Former Ranks of the Russian Corps, and offered its services to the United States government in the Korean War going on at that time. Although that offer was politely declined, it served notice to the American public that this group of Russians was firmly in the anti-Soviet camp.[5]

Colonel Rogozhin's main challenge as *Corpus* Commandant, however, was to seek help for those members already too ill or too old to work, and who looked to the *Corpus* to arrange food, shelter, and medical services. Those able to work therefore carried the dual burden of trying to find jobs in a new country where few knew the language, and at the same time supporting their less-able brothers-in-arms. Although most members came from the intelligentsia, the language barrier alone made it difficult to find work in any but low-skilled, low-paying jobs in the United States.

Poushental's offer was therefore seen as a Heaven-sent opportunity. Healthy *Corpus* veterans with a farming background (there were a few, mainly from the Cossack regiment) would work the farm. Profits would go toward acquiring and supporting a home for elderly veterans in Maine, where houses were cheap.

The 400-acre farm in Richmond posed the first serious problem in Maine for *Corpus* leaders. They had counted on it to become quickly self-supporting and to start generating an income stream. The leaders themselves, however, knew nothing about farming. Moreover, both Colonel Rogozhin and Major Cherepov, his deputy, continued to reside in New York City, where they had paying jobs. The difficulty in finding time to go to Richmond, which was a day's bus trip from New York, restricted their visits to one a month at most. Between such visits no one from the leadership was on hand to oversee operations on the farm, where three Cossack veterans had been hired to work.

Rogozhin soon realized, however, that farm operations were going badly. His report to the St. Alexander Nevsky Foundation, the *Corpus'* charitable offshoot, for 1952, the first year of operations, cited Maine's unprecedented drought that summer, followed by an early frost which caught the farm unprepared:

> It left all our crops in a wretched state, droopy and discolored. It has thus become clear to us that this place has an unusual climate, where planting cannot be done in June and July. That is knowledge for the future. But knowledge gained from shock is costly: we wasted both the labor and money spent on seed and plowing.[6]

Rogozhin's report noted that their land was nonetheless well-suited for farming—"that softened the bitter taste of failure," he said. Moreover, the autumn's hay-mowing had been a success, and discussions with local forestry experts had led to plans for cutting and selling the farm's timber—plans on which the *Corpus* leaders now pinned their hopes for making the farm profitable.

On a visit to the farm in March 1953, however, Rogozhin found that almost no timber had been cut. While attributing this in part to the workers' lack of tools—e.g., they had no power saws—he noted that

other farmers in the same neighborhood had cut timber this winter and apparently found it profitable. Unfortunately I realized too late that the manager of our farm was completely indifferent to the business of exploiting the timber. Of course I quickly dismissed him.[7]

As the farm's second planting season began, Rogozhin felt justified in deciding to continue its operations. If all went well and there was an "average" harvest, he said, then the thirty acres sown that spring should yield $5,000 in the fall. "Without a good harvest, however, the fall will find us without any money." Seeking to prepare the board members for this contingency, he noted that "according to its charter, the Foundation can do whatever seems appropriate with the property, including its sale . . ."[8] Moreover, he said, substantial repairs made to the house and barn had increased the property's value since Poushental had given it to them the year before.

The farm's second year of operations turned out, in fact, to be little better than the first. At the foundation's annual meeting in March 1954, a somber Rogozhin described how heavy spring rains and a summer drought had disrupted the grain crop, while the unexpected closure of a local cannery ended a promising market for the farm's vegetables after a one-time delivery of a thousand pounds of beans in midsummer. The season was again capped by an early frost which "seriously damaged all our crops." The farm's balance sheet for 1953 said it all: against an income of $1,600, its expenses came to around $5,000. Rogozhin concluded by announcing that it had thus become necessary "to give up the idea of developing agriculture on the estate and of making it a profitable enterprise." Salaries of the two workers had been ended in November 1953, and both began working "on shares to exploit our forest" which, with the help of hired labor, "we were convinced would at least cover expenses."[9]

In 1955 the foundation ended all its operations on the farm except haying. Its forest land was leased to a local timber firm which cut the wood for sale to a pulp mill. The farm was sold in 1958.

Meanwhile Colonel Rogozhin and other *Corpus* leaders had moved quickly to solicit membership dues ($25 a year) for the foundation's charitable activities, particularly the purchase of a home in Richmond for elderly *Corpus* veterans. By mid-1952 contributions from 240 *Corpus* members totaled almost $5,000. A half-dozen non-members, including Orthodox Bishop Nikon and Vladimir von Poushental, together contributed another $1,200.[10] The success in raising money made possible the purchase of a Richmond mansion in good condition in February 1953, only six months after the foundation had been chartered. The historic Southard mansion, built in 1855 by a wealthy local shipbuilder, had twelve rooms, two baths, and a three-car barn. As Rogozhin noted at the time of purchase, "The house is in the center of town, and a railway station is 50 steps away. The walk to our farm takes 30 to 40 minutes."[11]

Poushental, as broker, waived his sales commission on the house, which cost the foundation $4,050. The first resident moved in that spring. An Orthodox chapel, forerunner of the later St. Alexander Nevsky Church, was established in the mansion and consecrated in August 1953. A library was started at the same time. At the foundation's annual meeting in 1954 Rogozhin described the important role which the home was already playing among Maine's Russian-speaking residents: "It serves as the center of Russian social life in Maine. Its central location and its chapel attract all Russian Orthodox Christians living in the area."[12]

By that time the newly arrived Orthodox priest, his wife and three children, as well as three *Corpus* veterans, had moved into the home. One apartment was set aside for Rogozhin's personal use. To help pay maintenance costs, rooms were also let to guests for short stays. In 1956 a *Corpus* member bought a second Richmond house which he gave to the foundation. From 1956 until the early 1970s the foundation successfully maintained the two homes.

Lydia Rostov and her husband and two children were among the many *Corpus* families who rented suites in one or the other home during the summer. "We spent two weeks or more there every year between 1958 and 1970," she recalls. "We all cooked special Russian dishes to share with friends, and we made up our own entertainment." There was little mixing with non-*Corpus* people in the settlement, she says.

In 1972 Colonel Rogozhin died at the age of seventy-nine. This was a sad moment for the *Corpus*, which he had commanded since 1944 through war, internment, emigration, and resettlement. A man of gravitas and quiet dignity, Rogozhin is credited with keeping the *Corpus* intact and assuring its survival in the chaos of Central Europe at the end of World War II. Only his personal diplomatic demarche to Western military commanders had prevented the forced hand-over of the *Corpus* to Soviet military authorities to be executed like other Russian military groups that had served under the Germans.

By the early 1970s the foundation faced serious financial problems not of its own making. Thanks to members' dues and contributions, the foundation's books showed a credit balance of $15,000 in 1974, up a thousand from the year before. Expenses in caring for its growing ranks of needy, elderly members, however, were rising rapidly, while its rental income from the two homes remained flat. Between 1972 and 1974 the homes' annual expenses rose from $5,500 to $7,400, while their rental income stayed at around $4,000. Moreover, as Major Vertepov, the foundation's new president told its general meeting in 1975,

the oil crisis has sharply increased our costs of maintaining the homes. The situation has worsened with the declining number of paying residents. Rent no longer covers expenses . . . We have taken measures to raise the number of residents (including) an appeal in (the *Corpus* journal) urging members to move to Richmond.[13]

Efforts to attract more paying residents failed, however. The oil crisis, together with Richmond's continuing lack of the urban attractions to which most *Corpus* members and their families had by then grown accustomed, kept many from moving to Richmond. Older *Corpus* members who had visited there in the summer months gradually stopped coming as old friends died, or moved away to be with relatives living elsewhere. One of the foundation's homes was sold in the late 1970s. The main mansion, which housed only one tenant in its last years, closed its doors in 1982 and remained vacant until it was sold two years later.

Its closing brought to an end the *Corpus* presence in Maine. The farm and the two homes were gone, and the *Corpus* chapel had given way in 1960 to a new and separate parish church building constructed by St. Alexander Nevsky parishioners, many of whom had no ties to the *Corpus*. Neither the *Corpus* nor its St. Alexander Nevsky Foundation had established offices in Maine. Even the *Corpus'* commemorative chapel, a small but stunningly beautiful building, is located not in Maine, but in the cemetery of the Novo Divyevo Convent in Spring Valley, New York, where many *Corpus* members, including Colonel Rogozhin, and their families are buried. Despite its tenuous foothold in Maine, however, the *Corpus* homes and chapel there served as a nucleus and major attraction for Russian settlers and visitors all during the 1950s and 1960s, when it played a central role in the growth and life of the Russian Orthodox community. With Colonel Rogozhin's death in 1972 the *Corpus* moved its headquarters from New York to San Francisco, where its "young Cadets"—now in their seventies—have since assumed the leadership. The foundation's office remains in New York, where it still administers assistance to needy *Corpus* members, though on a much-reduced scale as death has taken a heavy toll of the "old émigré" generation. The *Corpus* no longer has any living members in the Richmond colony.

CHAPTER THREE

ACTING ON FAITH:
ALEXANDRA'S STORY

THE BLACK-AND-WHITE PHOTOGRAPH shows a beautiful woman of thirty-odd years with smoldering black eyes and the bobbed hair that was fashionable in the 1920s. "That is my mother. She was a coloratura soprano who sang with the Kiev opera. You see what dark eyes and hair she had? That's from her mother, who was Georgian. But my voice was not meant to sing opera." Over cups of tea in the dining room of her simple frame house in Richmond, Maine, Alexandra Sherbakoff leafs through photos and playbills kept in three albums, the record of the best years of her long and turbulent life: those involving dancing, singing, and the theater. In another photo a handsome young woman, slim and elegant, poses by the marble steps of a building. Her suit shows the flair and tailoring of a couturier. "That was taken in Belgrade around 1930. Someone from a Paris fashion house saw me dance and asked me to model in a show. I had never modeled before. But dancers naturally walk with grace, so they liked me. And I got to keep the suit." At eighty-eight Alexandra remains erect and carefully groomed, with a calm beauty, gentle voice, and graceful bearing.

She was born Alexandra Sposobskaya in Kiev, capital of the Ukraine, in 1911. Her grandfather had directed the construction of the Trans-Siberian railroad. "My father's family was wealthy, with homes in Kiev and St. Petersburg. He married my mother when she was sixteen. It was arranged by a matchmaker."

Alexandra saw little of her father. He continued to lead an active social life of his own, spending long periods away from Kiev. Like many upper-class Russians of that era, he had fairly open affairs with other women. "But my grandmother was very strict and very autocratic. When she found out that he was unfaithful to my mother, she forced a separation. So, when I was four years old, my mother and I went to live with my grandmother. My father refused to grant a divorce. He even came to Kiev to try to gain custody of me and bring me up among his family. My grandmother would not allow it."

By 1919, when Russia's civil war was raging across the country, Alexandra had acquired a stepfather as well as a sister, then four years old, born to her stepfather and her mother. The stepfather had served as an officer in the Tsar's army during the First World War. When the civil war began he joined one of the White armies organized in the Ukraine to fight the Bolsheviks. By 1920 the White forces were collapsing. Alexandra, together with her mother and sister, fled south in front of the army as it retreated toward the Black Sea port of Sevastopol.

Alexandra remembers the scene of chaos she witnessed there as a nine-year-old. "My mother went to search for my stepfather. I was left on the steps of the cathedral to look after my sister. There were crowds, people running and shouting, officers on horseback dashing about giving orders. It was a long time before my mother came back for us.

"We all waited there for my stepfather as long as we could. Then we were put on a ship going to Turkey. A few days later, in Istanbul, more of our troops and families showed up. One of the officers told us that my stepfather had boarded a ship at the last minute, but was told by someone that we were still waiting for him on a different wharf. So he got off the ship and went to look for us. By that time the fighting had spread to the port area, and my stepfather was killed."

The rest of the family, along with 75,000 other remnants of the White forces, ended up as refugees in Yugoslavia. At the start of their exile many in the Russian émigré colony looked forward to a quick collapse of the Bolshevik regime and an early return home. But as months and then years went by, the Russians settled in and created a Russian cultural environment in which to live and raise their families.

"We settled in the town of Novy Sad, in the old Hungarian region of Yugoslavia. My mother had to earn money to raise me and my two sisters—the youngest was born soon after we got there—so she sang with an operatic group that toured the country. From age ten to fourteen I did not go to school, but stayed home to take care of my sisters. I cooked and cleaned and hauled water in a bucket from the well. Then my mother married a Russian pilot who taught flying to Yugoslav air cadets. She and her husband moved to Belgrade. The apartment was too small for all three children to live with her. So she arranged for me to board at a Russian school, called a *realschule*, in Novy Sad."

The school was co-educational and academically rigorous, with advanced courses in science and math. Its director had graduated with honors from St. Petersburg's prestigious Smolny Institute, a school for bright daughters of the nobility. "So I also learned to speak beautiful Russian there. Our directress treated me like a daughter. Took me everywhere with her. There were even rumors that I *was* her daughter."

One of Alexandra's best friends at school was the daughter of Count Lamsdorf, a former diplomat and member of Hungary's old nobility. During a visit to the Lamsdorf country estate Alexandra received unexpected news of her father, whom she had neither seen nor heard from for a dozen years. "The first time I was invited to their home for a weekend our directress told me to wear the school dress uniform and behave as she had taught me. We got there in time for dinner and I was introduced to the Countess. Next morning I stayed inside while the others went out to play. The Countess came into the room, and I saw her looking at me intently. She motioned me to sit on a stool by her side. She asked, 'What's your name, child?' I said, 'Shura' (the diminutive of Alexandra). 'And where were you born, Shura?' 'Kiev.' 'Ah-ha,' she said. 'And what is your father's family name?' 'Sposobsky.' 'Ah, I knew it when I saw your eyes, Shura. I knew your father.' Without thinking, I blurted out 'Were you in love with him?' The Countess looked away, and didn't answer for a few moments. Finally she said, 'Shura, my marriage was arranged for me by my parents. That's the way things were done.' She hadn't answered directly, but I knew. Then she told me that my father had gone to Switzerland after the revolution. That was the first time I knew that he was even alive."

Alexandra turned out to be a prize student at the *realschule*. Under an intensified program designed for her by the director, she completed the entire *gymnasium* (high school) curriculum in three years instead of the usual seven. She shrugs off achievement. "I had a good memory," she says.

After graduation she joined her mother and sisters in Belgrade, where she began to explore her true interests: music and dance. "My dance teacher believed I had real potential for the ballet. So when Kersavina, a famous Russian ballet teacher from Paris, visited Belgrade, my teacher asked her to come and watch me dance. The woman liked my dancing, but she said, 'She's already too old to become a great ballerina. For that she should have begun training by age six, when the body is still flexible. But she can have great success performing national folk dances.' So that is what I studied, and that is what I stayed with."

Alexandra's future husband, Eugene Sherbakoff, was born in the Black Sea port of Odessa. "His great love was the theater," says Alexandra. "Even as a student at the local *gymnasium* he took courses at an actor's studio. When the First World War began he enrolled in a military school. He graduated as an officer and fought on the Eastern Front." During the civil war he joined a White Guards regiment and, like Alexandra and her family, fled to Yugoslavia following the Whites' defeat. There he took a law degree at a local university. "But that was just to get a degree, to have some sort of profession," Alexandra says. "He found a job as a telegrapher in Belgrade, and immediately joined the Russian Classic Theater Company."

The Company performed in the *Russkii Dom* (Russian House), the former Imperial Russian Consulate. Its theater, concert hall, and library became the cultural center for the Russian émigré community in the 1920s and 1930s. Eugene came to be well-known for his acting under the stage name "E. Yevgenev." He also belonged to a traveling group of actors, singers, and dancers. "They called themselves

'Carousel,' because they went round and round from one city to another to perform," says Alexandra.

Alexandra and Eugene first met in 1927. She was seventeen and he was thirty-two. "He came to our house one day to call on my mother. She asked me to serve tea. But this man kept staring at me and whispering to my mother, so I left the room. Soon she called me back in, remarking on my rudeness. It turned out that Carousel had asked him to find a young dancer to join their company in time for a two-week tour in Croatia. My mother said no, I was too young. But he persisted, and finally she agreed to let me join them, but only for those two weeks.

"As the tour ended I was of course hoping to stay with the group. But before we returned to Belgrade a letter arrived from my mother saying I must come home. Eugene saw me crying, and asked what had happened. I showed him the letter. He said nothing. The next day he was missing from rehearsal, and a member of the troop laughed and said he had gone to see his mother-in-law. I had not heard that he was married. When he came back that evening he handed me another letter from my mother. She wrote Eugene had been to see her, that he wanted to marry me, and that she had given her permission! So he was not married after all! I was already in love with him . . . he was such a big, handsome man, and everyone liked him. Of course I accepted his proposal."

Alexandra then became a permanent member of Carousel and performed with the company "every night of the week except when we were on a train between cities." In the early 1930s, after they had been on the road several years, the chance came for a more settled professional and personal life. "A friend of Eugene's named Strakhov, a musician who made a good living translating and adapting Western musicals for Serbian audiences, had seen our group perform. He liked us and suggested that we locate in a permanent theater—a former cabaret that was available in Belgrade. And so the Krokodil Theater was born, with Strakhov as producer and Eugene as director."

Alexandra describes how Strakhov's sense of showmanship brought a major change in the staging of her performances. "My singing had always been done simply, without special costumes or lighting. Then this Strakhov told Eugene I should have more dramatic settings for my songs and dances. And what changes he made! You know what he did?" Alexandra raises her eyebrows in mock surprise and drops her voice in hushed intimacy. "For my song 'Bublichki,' a simple story of a young girl selling hot rolls, he had the rest of the cast stroll through the market place, humming as they shop. Then the lights slowly dim, the crowd begins to leave, and the market people close down their stalls for the day. As the stage empties, I enter as a poor peasant girl with her basket of rolls for sale, but of course she is soon all alone, no one to buy them. Very sad. But *very* dramatic."

Publicity stills from Alexandra's days in the Krokodil Theatre show a young woman of vibrant beauty. Her fine dark hair is long and parted in the center. Long, arching eyebrows and dark lashes give an intensity to her ice-blue eyes. The nose is long and straight, the lips a cupid's bow reminiscent of silent film actresses. A strong chin and jaw-line add character to the face. In most of the pictures her face is framed by elaborate ethnic headdresses—a jeweled Ukrainian tiara in one, a Georgian pillbox hat and veil in another—and her features seem to change in each. Eugene had moments of at least feigned professional jealousy toward Alexandra. "After one of my perfor-mances I asked him, 'How did you like my singing?' and he said, 'Oh, I didn't notice the singing. I was listening to your accompanist.'"

By her mid-twenties Alexandra, performing under the name "Alexandra Nevskaya" after a revered Russian warrior-saint, was known throughout Yugoslavia as a dancer and singer of ballads. She had made records and sung over Radio Belgrade. Yet she had never performed alone before a live audience. She has a vivid recollection of the first occasion. "One day my husband got a call from the wife of a Yugoslav cabinet minister. She wanted me to sing and dance in a benefit performance for Russian veterans of the Great War. It was to take place in a grand hotel in Herseg Novi, a town on the Adriatic coast near Dubrovnik. A large group of former Tsarist officers, all elderly, lived in a rented house there, and they were running out of money to pay the rent.

"I was very nervous. I knew that high-ranking Yugoslav officers and diplomats would be in the audience. I was met at the train by some local Russian émigrés who were to be my hosts. They drove me to the hotel, a beautiful white villa, where the concert was to take place. A garden overlooked the Adriatic, with marble steps going down to the sea. It was May, and magnolia and oleander were in bloom.

"I sang three songs, accompanied by a Yugoslav military orchestra . . . I wasn't used to such *strong* accompaniment, but they played softly. Then I performed three dances—Hungarian, Gypsy, and Russian—appearing in a different costume for each. For the last my headdress was a heavy golden helmet. After the performance the commander of the Yugoslav fleet kissed my hand and led me in a waltz, while everyone applauded. And I was given huge bouquets. Then everyone danced. Later the admiral led me to a table loaded with jewelry and other personal valuables which the sponsors had donated to be raffled off to raise money for the veterans. He said, 'Take any of the jewels you want. They're yours.' I said, 'No, I won't do that. But I would like to have that doll in Russian national dress.' He smiled and said, 'Somehow I knew you would choose that.'

"I was tired, so I went to my changing-room and lay down for a while, surrounded by my flowers, including sprays of oleander and magnolia. I immediately fell asleep. My host's wife woke me. She quickly opened the windows and removed the flowers. She said, 'Thank God, you're all right! Don't you know that magnolia and oleander give off a poisonous scent? With all the windows shut like that, you could have died of suffocation.'"

A few years ago a local friend of Alexandra's visited her before leaving on a trip to Yugoslavia's Adriatic coast. "I asked her, 'Please, when you go there, stop in at Herseg Novi Monastery, and light a candle for the Russian veterans buried in its cemetery. And visit the cemetery for me.' But do you know, when she came home she told me, 'Alexandra, I visited the cemetery. But there are no Russian graves there now. They are gone.' It made me very sad. All those people, and nothing to remember them by."

World War II brought a sudden end to the Sherbakoffs' shimmering lives as émigré artists in Yugoslavia. In 1942, following the German conquest of that country, the Russian émigrés felt threatened from all sides. Those men ready to serve in the German-organized *Russkii Corpus* put pressure on other émigrés—particularly on former Tsarist officers like Eugene—to join. He refused. "He said 'I swore allegiance to the Tsar. I will not disgrace myself by putting on a German uniform,'" says Alexandra. His refusal, however, led to hostility on the part of some *Corpus* members, who spread the rumor that he was a Jew. Fearing that the Germans would hear that rumor and believe it, Eugene decided to leave Yugoslavia and seek work in Germany. Alexandra would remain in Belgrade, where she at least had her mother and stepfather, a *Corpus* member himself, to protect her.

But Alexandra soon found her own life threatened—in her case by Yugoslavs who suspected her of pro-German sympathies. "It happened like this. One day a Nazi officer knocked on the door of the apartment, saying he wanted to talk with me. I had to let him in, of course. 'I have heard that you are a beautiful singer and dancer,' he told me. 'We want you to perform for our German soldiers.' I said, 'Oh, thank you very much, but unfortunately I don't sing any more. I strained my voice and I have chronic laryngitis.' 'Well, in that case,' he said, 'you must bring me a doctor's certificate stating that fact.'

"As soon as he left I went out to see my doctor and to ask if he would give me such a thing. But as I left, the building superintendent stopped me. 'Why was that Nazi officer visiting you?' I told him the whole story, but he didn't believe me. He accused me of being a Nazi collaborator, and said, 'If you come back, you will not get out of here alive.' So I went right to my mother's apartment, leaving everything behind. Later, when I finally heard from Eugene and had his address in Germany, I went to join him. But I didn't know that we would be doing forced labor there." She and Eugene were put to work in a factory near Breslau, which turned out heavy spools of thread. "We were of course separated from each other. But we met occasionally on our way to or from work and would talk together through a wire fence."

The hard work, the cold, and the meager food given forced laborers weakened Alexandra. A severe bout of pleurisy led to her transfer to a home for ill and mostly very poor people where faulty treatment only worsened her condition. The home provided only the crudest medical services. "There was a nurse, but no doctor. The first thing she did was draw a vial of blood from my arm. 'Oh, you have good veins, lots of blood,' she said. 'That's needed for our wounded German soldiers.' Then she stuck a big needle in my shoulder, and drew a liter of water from my lungs.

"So I grew weaker. Eugene didn't know where I was. Then after a few weeks a doctor, a real doctor, made his rounds one day and examined me. He spoke Russian and talked about the Ukraine, where he had studied. He arranged for me to stay in a hospital for a month on extra rations and ordered me put on light work afterwards." Alexandra believes that God must have sent that sympathetic doctor to her; otherwise she says she would have died. When she returned to the factory, however, the authorities assigned her to heavy work again. Afraid to protest, Alexandra soon developed pneumonia. Instead of returning her to the hospital, the plant's officials placed her in what she calls a "transit hostel"—a building where extremely ill Russian POWs and forced workers were installed without any medical attention.

By then it was the winter of 1944-45, and the final Soviet offensive was causing confusion and a rapid breakdown in the German administration. "I was too sick to be aware of what was going on around me. Eventually Eugene found out where I was. Meanwhile he received a letter from an actor named Cheropil who had been in the Krokodil company. How it found its way to us we never knew. He wrote that a group of these people, twenty-six of them, had somehow survived, and were living in the mountains near Carlsbad. Cheropil urged us to come to them." Taking advantage of the growing chaos in eastern Germany, Eugene made plans to rescue Alexandra from the hostel and flee with her to join their old friends. "Through a Latvian friend who worked for the railroad, Eugene got two tickets on a train that went to Carlsbad. It was winter. Eugene came for me in the night, covered me with a blanket, and put me on a sled. I was only half-conscious . . . he pulled me through the streets to the station, and carried me into the train." Alexandra remembers little of that trip or of the weeks that followed. They found their friends and, together, discussed what they should do. Soviet troops would soon occupy the area. Since the Sherbakoffs and the others had all sided with the Whites in the civil war and were thus among the earliest opponents of Communism, their overriding concern was to avoid falling into Soviet hands.

"We decided to try to reach Munich, which we had heard was occupied by the Americans. We boarded a train going in that direction, but it was forced to stop at a village, Diezenhof, about a half-hour from Munich. There was no place to stay. Even the town mayor couldn't help us. And you know, we were a strange group of Russians, and the Red Army was known to be coming . . . the local people maybe thought we were spies, who knows? The rest of the group decided to go on by foot. But it was so cold, and I was too weak to walk.

"On the edge of the village Eugene and I found a bombed-out warehouse to stay in . . . only a couple of walls still standing. We traded some of our clothes for wood and a tarpaulin to cover us. We traded more of our things to a local farmer for food—a pail of milk and a turnip. And the next day three potatoes, which Eugene cooked over a fire. There was no other food to be found, so that farmer truly saved our lives."

Over the next couple of days other refugees fleeing west joined them in the warehouse. They brought reports of advancing Soviet troops only a few days behind them. Since Alexandra was by then a little stronger, she and Eugene bundled up their few remaining belongings and trekked toward Munich and the Americans.

United States troops there had already set up camps to house and feed Displaced Persons—i.e., non-German refugees. "But I told Eugene, 'No more camps.' We met a Russian family staying in an old abandoned house. So he left me there while he went to find work with the Americans. Late that day he overheard two officers talking. One said he was looking for a chef. Eugene said, 'I can cook.' So he and the officer got in a jeep and drove across the city to a large residence which the Americans had taken over. But I didn't know any of this. Evening came, and no Eugene. I was worried. Late at night a jeep drove up, and Eugene brought me some food. He said, 'I've got to get back right away, but I'll see you tomorrow.' And off he went in the jeep. The next two days a soldier in a jeep brought food, but no Eugene.

"The third evening a jeep came again, and again no Eugene. The driver said, 'Your husband wants you to come right away. He's got work for you.' I grabbed a few musical scores I had saved and put on the nicest clothes I had left so I could be ready to sing. The jeep drove up to this big house, and the driver took me to the kitchen. There was Eugene preparing food for a large group of officers. He pointed to a sink full of dirty pots and pans, and said, 'Hurry up, those need to be washed.' That was the work he had for me!"

For the next two years the Sherbakoffs had charge of the house, in which a dozen U.S. Army officers were billeted. Eugene was chef and Alexandra the head housekeeper. The Americans came to like and trust the Sherbakoffs. When the billet was closed and the officers left for the United States, however, Eugene and Alexandra had no choice but to move into a camp for Displaced Persons.

There they met a wealthy American who was looking for a couple to live with his elderly parents in New York City. He sponsored the Sherbakoffs as immigrants, bringing them to the United States in 1948. On arrival they were surprised to be met by several of the Americans they had known in Munich, some coming from as far away as Texas to see them.

But there were problems. "Unfortunately our sponsor's mother died before we even went to work for them. He invited us instead to come work in *his* home, a large duplex apartment in Manhattan." Alexandra's congenital heart condition, made worse by her stay in the German labor camp, quickly flared up. "My legs swelled from going up and down the steep stairs in that apartment. So Eugene told the man we just could not do all the things required of us, and would have to look for other work. He understood, and said we could stay in the apartment for two weeks while he and his wife went on vacation in the Bahamas."

Meanwhile Eugene had already become involved in the Master Institute, a classic Russian theater on West 103rd Street in Manhattan. Its managing director, Zelitsky, was a well-known Russian actor and director who had studied at the prestigious Second Studio of the Moscow Theater until his defection in mid-1930s. He knew of Eugene's work in Belgrade, and was eager to have his help in reviving classic Russian plays in New York.

"The day after we knew we must leave the duplex, Zelitsky introduced Eugene to a man representing a group of Russian Jews who held weekend retreats at a country house outside the city. They were interested in having plays performed there. They talked for a while, and when this man learned we had no place to live, he offered us rooms in his house—an offer which Eugene immediately accepted."

A few weeks later Sherbakoff, Zelitsky, and other actors from the Master Theater went to the Sabbath retreat to perform. Alexandra went along. "Suddenly and unexpectedly I was asked to sing. I had no scores with me, I hadn't practiced. But I sang. Next morning Zelitsky handed me an envelope. In it was a thank-you note and a hundred-dollar bill from a man named Blumenthal who was the local representative of Arpel Jewellers."

Over the next decade the classic Russian theater flourished, though on a shoestring. Eugene was instrumental, both as director and actor, in bringing about its revival. Alexandra leafs through her album's dozen or more photographs of plays performed in those years, pointing out famous Russian theater people who were involved. "We had some truly great artists—Khelmetsky the playwright; Rybakova, who played Anna in *Anna Karenina*; Smolyakov the ballet dancer; Bastunov, a famous actor from the Moscow stage. But here in the States all that didn't count for much. They were not known to the American public; few of them spoke English well. So all of them had to work during the day at other jobs, mostly menial, and rehearse at night. Sometimes rehearsals went on until two in the morning."

Alexandra had neither a good command of English at that time nor name recognition in the United States theater and entertainment world, thus ruling out a professional career in her adoptive land. Her name was well known, however, among the Russian émigré community, which called on her to perform at several prestigious events. One was the 1948 *Morskii Vecher* (Navy Evening) a gala affair to benefit Tsarist naval veterans that was held, appropriately, in New York's Empire Hotel. Alexandra was one of a half-dozen artists featured in a program that included a talk by Countess Tolstoy, daughter of the great writer, Leo Tolstoy. The Countess was well known in her own right, as a writer and as founder of the Tolstoy Farm, a private reception center for Russian refugees which she herself ran.

Alexandra worked days in an Automat cafeteria—"My food was free and always fresh"—and later on the production line of the Coty cosmetics firm. Eugene worked for an organization that delivered food and clothing from Russian immigrants to their relations in the U.S.S.R. Yet they found time to take part in many performances. "We did so many plays . . . Gogol's *Inspector-General*, and adaptations from his *Dead Souls* and Dostoevsky's *Brothers Karamazov*. We did Chekhov and Ostrovsky and Yevgenev as well." Her photos of live performances show Eugene in various leading roles and herself as both actress and singer. Close-ups of her husband show astonishing facial transformations from role to role. "Yes, he always insisted on doing his own make-up. He was good at it."

Meanwhile Alexandra had located her mother and her two half-sisters, none of whom she had seen or heard from since leaving Belgrade in 1942. "I had no idea how to reach them, whether they had survived the war, anything. But soon after we came here some of our American friends from Munich offered to help. I gave them my mother's old Belgrade address, which they wired to the American consul. He went to the apartment, and found her still living there!

"My mother wrote a long letter telling me what had happened to them during the eight years we were separated. She was widowed early in the war, and had married another Russian émigré. Both sisters were married, and Iraida, the older one, had a young son." Over the next several years Alexandra and Eugene sent regular packages of food and clothing to her family. By the mid-1950s, with help from the Sherbakoffs, all of them had come to the United States. "My mother arrived first. I met her at the boat, but so did her husband. He had arrived in the U.S. earlier, and had a job at the Tolstoy Farm. He took her right from the boat to the Farm . . . I hardly had a chance to talk with her!" The two sisters and their husbands reached the States a little later and settled in New Jersey, where they all found work.

By 1958 Alexandra's health was deteriorating. Her doctor said she should move out of New York City to a more healthful environment. She and Eugene decided to settle in Richmond, where they had friends among its growing colony of Russian-speaking immigrants. Both found work—Eugene part-time in a bakery and as a private caterer, Alexandra on the production line in a local factory. There she first felt discrimination as a Russian. "When I went to apply, the manager said, 'No, we have no jobs.' Then a neighbor of ours, a non-Russian working there, spoke up. 'Oh, I know Alexandra. She's all right.' So I got the job." It was piecework, starting at ten cents, which brought her about six dollars a day. When she retired eighteen years later she was earning twelve cents.

Within a few months of their move to Richmond Eugene and Alexandra organized a group to produce and perform Russian music and drama. In July 1958 their first performance in Maine—two one-act comedies and a selection of Russian songs—was presented to a local audience. Their group was small: the Sherbakoffs, a Russian artist named Belenkov and his wife, and one or two others from the Russian colony. Occasionally a visiting singer or actor, usually one of the Sherbakoffs' former colleagues from the Master Theater in New York, would take part.

"Our performances were in Russian, of course. So, when we played for non-Russian audiences a synopsis of each piece and some-thing about its author and its social significance would be given beforehand in English. We were fortunate to have Lydia Rennen-kampf to do this. She was the daughter of a famous Russian general. And she spoke beautiful English." After a year or so the group was receiving invitations to perform at nearby colleges and for other audi-ences around the Kennebec Valley. Eugene also served as a director and consultant with the Augusta Players in Maine's capital and with college drama groups at Bowdoin College and at the University of Maine. The Sherbakoffs took an active interest in other aspects of Russian community life as well. Eugene's outgoing personality, together with fluency in English, enabled him to form easy friend-ships among the town's non-Russian residents. He often found him-self called upon as an informal advisor and interpreter, particularly for elderly Russians who spoke little or no English and who found American ways and institutions baffling. Some of the Russian settlers asked him to run for selectman to represent their interests before the town. He refused, instead urging them to support a young non-Russian who knew more about town affairs and who would, he felt, represent the settlers' interests fairly.

Both Eugene and Alexandra were troubled by the lack of cohesion and cooperation among the Russian-speaking settlers, and by their social isolation. "Some were very old," Alexandra recalls. "Only a few had cars, and they lived on scattered farms that were several miles outside the town. So Eugene organized a little community center: a rented house in town where they could sit and drink tea from a *samovar* and read Russian-language newspapers when they came into town for supplies. The rent was $40 a month. Eugene and I put in $10, my mother and sister, who were living here by then, each contributed $10, and the others contributed fifty cents each. Well, it lasted two years. There were suspicions at first over what we were 'really' going to do, et cetera. And then complaints, always complaints. You know what? Some of those people said they should be receiving groceries, too, for their fifty-cent contributions! So sad." Eugene also served on a committee to raise pension money for older immigrants, but that, too, failed for want of support.

Some of the Sherbakoffs' friends, particularly among the First Wave émigrés, were—like Alexandra and Eugene—distressed that there was so little sense of *obschina* (community) among the settlers. Alexandra recalls conversations between her husband and Colonel Anatoli Rogozhin, commandant of the *Corpus*. "He was such a fine man. He often came to our house to talk with Eugene. He would mention some problem, then say, 'Eugene, what's *wrong* with the Russian people here? Why can't they get together and agree on anything?' And Eugene would tell him, 'Look, they're Ukrainians and Belorussians and Cossacks as well as Russians. And they all want to do different things, and do them in their own way. *That's* the problem.' And you know, Eugene was right."

Yet Alexandra feels that ethnic frictions and suspicions were compounded by other, even deeper differences, especially those between First Wave émigrés like the Sherbakoffs, who had never lived under the Soviet regime, and those of the Second Wave, who had. "Many people who left Russia later, even in the early 1940s, had spent most of their lives under Communism. That gave them an entirely different viewpoint, an entirely different attitude toward life and people. It made them so fearful, so suspicious."

She tells of a young Russian woman who left the Soviet Union around 1980. "The girl came to stay with me for a while, and we became good friends. One day she said to me, 'You are so different from us, Alexandra. You always say what you think. We learned to say what we do *not* think, and to think what we do not say. You trust everyone. We trust no one. When I was a child my parents drilled me to forget anything they talked about at home. So when our teachers asked us to report what our parents said, I always told them my parents were busy people and never talked to me much.' That girl made me see just how wide the differences are between the old émigrés, like me, and those who left later."

Alexandra became an active and involved member of the St. Alexander Nevsky Church, which is six village blocks from her house. She assists the Orthodox equivalent of an altar guild, responsible for keeping vestments, candelabra, and other church paraphernalia in good condition and preparing the altar for services. Both she and her husband were particularly supportive of each of the several successive parish priests, helping them to find housing, move their household belongings, and get settled.

Both Alexandra and Eugene, however, stayed out of the politics and personality clashes that brought occasional dissension to Richmond's Russian Orthodox community. Nor did they have close ties to the *Corpus*, whose members had founded the church and who generally favored the restoration of the monarchy under Great Russian hegemony. "Eugene said, 'I fought for the Tsar once. But that was a long time ago. The Tsar is dead,'" says Alexandra. "He said, 'What do *we* know about what's going on in the U.S.S.R.? It's up to the people there to decide what they want.'" Although Alexandra, like her late husband, shows no political leaning toward restoring Russia's monarchy, she keeps a tinted photograph of Tsar Nicholas II and his family among the mementos of old Russia that line the tops of her dining-room buffet and china cabinet.

During their fourteen years together in Richmond, Eugene and Alexandra made friends among their neighbors and other non-Russians in the town. Since Eugene's death in 1972, Alexandra has continued to welcome and maintain such contacts, even in her eighties. She is widely known and liked in Richmond, where her non-Russian friends have abbreviated her name to "Sandy."

Her closest friend in town—the only one with whom she can be "entirely open," she says—is a Russian woman. "But it's not the same," meaning that the truly close friend in her life was Eugene. "My life came to an end when he died. One still has to live. But I lost all interest in shopping, buying clothes, caring how I looked." She glances about the room, at the furniture, the pictures, the icons. Except for votive candles burning in memory of her husband and her mother, "All these things are just as they were when Eugene died twenty-two years ago. He did most of the furnishing and decorating, since I was too busy working. So in this room I'm surrounded by my life, my memories. This was our first and only house."

Alexandra has nonetheless remained an active and engaged woman—strong-willed and intensely involved with the things that interest her. In spite of her weak heart and the occasional bouts of arthritis and bursitis, she continues to do her own cooking and housework as well as caring for a cat, a variety of house plants, and a flower garden which she herself seeds, weeds, and feeds. Until suffering a broken hip in an auto accident in September 1994, Alexandra drove a car, took elderly friends grocery-shopping, and regularly attended services at St. Alexander Nevsky Church.

The broken hip she viewed as a temporary setback, not a life-changing disaster. She was intrigued by the technology of her surgery. "The nurse told me a six-inch pin had been screwed into my hip. I said, 'Oh, my—*that* big?' And she said, 'Well, some people have them *this* long'—and she held out her hands two feet apart!" A friend who visited her in the hospital shortly after her surgery found that her greatest concern was her pet cat. "How will he get fed? I must get home." A few days later a visitor found her inching her way painfully along the crowded hospital corridor, pushing a walker before her. "I must put seventy-five percent of my weight on the good leg, and twenty-five percent on the other one," she explained. To the amazement of the surgeon and physical therapist, who had urged her to spend time in a convalescent center, she was home, engaging in normal activities with the aid of a walker and long-handled pickup tongs, two weeks after the surgery. A year later she was driving again. She was eighty-three at the time.

There is a deeply reflective, mystical side to Alexandra. Her faith in God has clearly been reinforced by her survival of danger, adversity, and loneliness: narrow escape from Russia during the civil war; a lonely childhood followed by an unexpected career on the stage and a happy marriage; flight to the safety and security of U. S. lines after the frightening war years of illness, hunger, and forced labor; peaceful and contented married life in America, where she was reunited with her mother and sisters. Acknowledging that she herself had virtually no control over these events, Alexandra gives God full credit for the positive outcomes. "Nothing happens accidentally," she says. "I always pray to God. Nothing formal . . . just 'Please, God, help me.' And He always has."

Alexandra's strong faith also shows in the detailed attention she has given to burial arrangements and subsequent Orthodox observances at the graves of her mother, sister, and husband, all of whom lie buried in the cemetery of the Novo Divyevo Convent in Spring Valley, New York. When Ludmilla, the sister to whom she was especially close, died in 1994, Alexandra made the 370-mile trip to Novo Divyevo to oversee (and pay for) the funeral arrangements and attend the burial service. She also saw to the disposition of Ludmilla's belongings, nearly all of which she donated to the Convent. In accord with Orthodox custom, Alexandra remained in heavy mourning for the next forty days. On the fortieth day she again made the long drive with friends to Spring Valley, where she had arranged for the all-important Orthodox *panikhida* service at Ludmilla's grave. Put in its simplest terms, the *panikhida* is the final farewell, marking the departure of the spirit to its permanent resting-place. The service took place in July, on a still day when the temperature and humidity broke 90 degrees. Alexandra, swathed in black, stood alert and erect in the hot sun, giving oral responses as the priest and *Matushka*, the Mother Superior of the Convent, chanted the service. Later Alexandra and her friends walked about the cemetery to visit the graves of her other family members. Later still, according to Orthodox custom, she took her friends to dinner in Ludmilla's memory. It was the first solid food Alexandra had tasted in forty days. Back home she put away her mourning clothes and changed into a light summer dress.

In the autumn Alexandra received a check from Ludmilla's burial insurance policy. She had already decided how to use it. "I want a raised border of stones placed around her grave, and stones on top so that it can be easily maintained." She later recalled a dream she had had before Ludmilla's death. "You know, it was while she was ill in hospital. I dreamed that I heard a sound from my garden. And when

I looked out, some men were digging a hole there. They looked up and said, 'Don't worry. It's not for you.' Then I woke up. I see now that dream was telling that Ludmilla would die."

On another occasion Alexandra recounted a dream that held still greater meaning for her. "The other night I could not sleep, my heart was pounding. Then I had this dream about Eugene. He came to my room and motioned to me to come with him. We went down the steps . . . it was raining very hard outside. Then he walked off in one direction, and I walked in another. As I watched, he grew smaller and smaller in the distance. So I think, God is not ready for me to follow Eugene just yet."

PHOTOGRAPHS

I. Aerial photograph of Richmond Center,
St. Alexander Nevsky Church and Southard mansion in center foreground.
Photograph by Lloyd Ferris. Courtesy of the Richmond Historical and Cultural Society.

II. View of Richmond Center, corner of South Front Street and Main Street. Galleried
building on right was a *Russkii Corpus* house for veterans and summer visitors.
Photographer unknown. Courtesy of the Richmond Historical and Cultural Society.

III. Baron Vladimir von Poushental after a day's shooting, 1950.
Photographer unknown. Courtesy of Day Kokarev Jr.

IV. Baron Vladimir von Poushental and hunting companions, 1950.
Photographer unknown. Courtesy of Day Kokarev Jr.

V. Poushenthal among the hunting trophies in his Pittston chalet, late 1960s.
From *Kennebec Journal*, 1 April 1981. Photographer unknown.

KENNEBEC REALTY Inc.

For Sale:
Land Lots, Chicken and other farms,
City and Country houses etc..
also
Listing for sale: houses, farms,
and other Land properties
Appraisals and Consultations, apply
for informations.
Telephones:

Русская контора по продаже земельных
участков, куриных и прочих ферм, городс-
ких и дачных домов и прочих видов недвижимой собственности.
Также принимаем на комиссию все
виды недвижимой собственности,
даем бесплатно советы по продаже
и го приобретению недвижимостей
За справками и информацией обра-
щайтесь по телефону или лично:

737-4959 or 582-3917

VI. Poushental's Kennebec Realty, Inc. sign in front of Southard mansion, 1950s.
Photographer unknown. Courtesy of the Richmond Historical and Cultural Society.

VII. Colonel Rogozhin (in white), his daughter, and *Russkii Corpus* members welcome Father George Gorsky, first parish priest of St. Alexander Nevsky Church, with the traditional bread and salt, 1953. Photograph by Freeda Witham.

VIII. Father George Gorsky conducts Maine's first Russian Orthodox mass, St. Alexander Nevsky Chapel in Southard mansion, October 1953. Photograph by Freeda Witham.

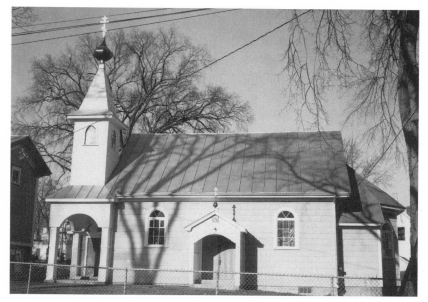

IX. St. Alexander Nevsky Church, Church Street, Richmond, about 1960.
Photograph by Freeda Witham.

X. Interior of St. Alexander Nevsky Church, about 1960.
Photograph by Freeda Witham.

XI. Southard mansion, Church Street, Richmond, home for *Russkii Corpus* veterans and site of first St. Alexander Nevsky Church: Maine's first Russian Orthodox place of worship, 1950s. Photograph by Freeda Witham.

XII. *Russkii Corpus* "Anti-Communist Meeting on Free Russia," May 1958. Speakers included Orthodox Bishop Nikon (center) and *Corpus* head Col. Rogozhin (second from left). Ivan Sitchenko, *ataman* of the local Cossacks, is at far left. The "PK" at the center of the cross in the foreground is the symbol of the *Russkii Corpus*.

XIII. Father Chad Williams, parish priest of St. Alexander Nevsky Church since 1987.
Courtesy of Father Chad Williams.

XIV. Alexandra Sherbakoff in Ukrainian folkdance costume, 1930s.
Courtesy of Alexandra Sherbakoff.

XV. Alexandra Sherbakoff as a Georgian folkdancer, 1930s.
Courtesy of Alexandra Sherbakoff.

XVI. Eugene Sherbakoff consulting with Brunswick Music Theater actors
Larry Brooks and Willie Burke in "A Song for Anastasia."
From Brunswick *Times-Record*, February 13, 1964.

XVII. Alexandra serving Eugene tea from samovar, 1968.
Courtesy of Alexandra Sherbakoff.

XVIII. Professor Pavel Vaulin at University of South Alabama, early 1970s.
Courtesy of Pavel Vaulin.

XIX. Pavel Vaulin at home, summer 1996.
Photograph by Robert Jaster.

XX. Pavel Vaulin outside his "fortress," 1996.
Photograph by Robert Jaster.

XXI. Cossack celebration of *pokrová*, 1963.
The painting shows the Virgin holding the mystical cloak. From left: Tanya Petrochenko,
companion to Ivan Sitchenko; Father Afanasi Donetskoy, ex-Cossack and Tsarist officer;
Lydia Rennenkampf, daughter of a famous Russian general in World War I;
and Ivan Sitchenko, *ataman* of the local Cossacks.

ВЫДАЧА КАЗАКОВ В ЛИЕНЦЕ
АВСТРИЯ — ИЮНЬ 1945

LA TRAHISON DES COSAQUES A LIENZ
AUTRICHE, JUIN 1945

BETRAYAL OF COSSACKS AT LIENZ
AUSTRIA, JUNE 1945

Работа художника С. Г. Королько...
Painting by S. G. Korolkoff

...E AUSLIEFERUNG DER KOSAKEN IN LIENZ
OESTERREICH, JUNI 1945

Фотография Н. Телятникова
Photo by N. Teliatnikow

XXII. *Betrayal of the Cossacks at Lienz*, Austria, June 1945.
Reprint of a picture in *Soglasie*, bulletin of the *Russkii Corpus*.

XXIII. Daniel Boochko as "Cossack," Richmond Days Parade, late 1970s.
Photograph by Andy Krochmaluk.

XXIV. Basilio Lepuschenko, 1983.
Courtesy of Anna Sidelinger.

XXV. Nick Arkas, 1996.
Photograph by Robert Jaster.

XXVI. Nick Arkas's father and grandfather outside family *dasha* in Bogdanovka, Ukraine, 1908. Courtesy of Nick Arkas.

XXVII. Nick Arkas's grandfather, admiral in Russian navy, about 1900.
Courtesy of Nick Arkas.

XXVIII. Nick Arkas's great grandfather, Commander of the Black Sea fleet, 1870s.
Courtesy of Nick Arkas.

XXIX. Yelena Schumejko (far left) as a mermaid in production of "Golden Lake," a Russian fairytale, 1959.Other "mermaids" in photo are Olga Taranko, Anna Wdowin, and Tamara Wdowin. Photograph by Freeda Witham.

XXX. Yelena Schumejko outside her new house in Richmond, 1996. Photograph by Robert Jaster.

XXXI. Anna Sidelinger in her office in Gardiner Savings Bank, Richmond, 1996.
Photograph by Robert Jaster.

XXXII. Michail Grizkewitsch.
Courtesy of Michail Grizkewitsch.

XXXIII. Russian farmer Boris Dulkin and his animals, early 1960s.
Photograph by Freeda Witham.

XXXIV. Staged photograph of Russian farmer Boris Dulkin with goat, early 1960s.
Photograph by Freeda Witham.

XXXV. Day Kokarev Sr. (center) as a Tsarist soldier in World War I, 1917.
Courtesy of Day Kokarev Jr.

XXXVI. Day Kokarev Sr. as Baptist Minister, 1959.
Courtesy of Day Kokarev Jr.

XXXVII. Nikodin Belenkov with two of his paintings, 1958.
Photograph by Freeda Witham.

XXXVIII. Princess Vera Romanoff with Captain Gregory Mesnaeff, head of
Russian Cadet Corps veterans, Richmond, 1958.
Photograph by Freeda Witham.

XXXIX. Michael Agapow working in his Russian boot shop, 1960.
Photograph by Freeda Witham.

XL. Russian children performing for Russian library benefit, 1959.
Photograph by Freeda Witham.

XLI. Russian children's Christmas celebration in church, 1953.
Photograph by Freeda Witham.

XLII. Russian children in Christmas play, 1972.
Photograph by Freeda Witham.

PART TWO

Some of [Richmond's First Wave immigrants] looked down on us [Second Wave people], and said we were Communists since we had lived in the U.S.S.R. during the 1930s. They didn't know how badly Stalin treated the Cossacks. We had no love for Stalin. But what could we do?

–Lara Razko, personal interview, 1995

CHAPTER FOUR

METAMORPHOSIS OF LT. PETUKHOV:
PAVEL'S STORY

PAVEL VAULIN IS A MAN OF STRONG CONVICTIONS strongly expressed. As his first political act, at age thirteen he punched a local Communist Party organizer in the nose, knocking him down. "This young man came to our village and spoke against the farmers as 'enemies of the people.' I got mad at what he said, the lies he told about our people."

Looking at Pavel sixty years later it is easy to imagine him as a tough, combative teenager ready to punch out an opponent. He has the spare, wiry build of a boxer, and the agility of a man thirty years younger. He is of medium height, with wavy gray hair, a concave Slav nose, and deep-set blue eyes that are alert and challenging. Yet his normally serious, brooding expression can give way suddenly to a grin or quiet laugh in conversation.

He was born Pavel Petukhov in 1918 to a farm family in the Ural Mountains that separate Russia proper from Siberia. The nearest city, Sverdlovsk, was a hundred miles away. Recently reverting to its pre-Soviet name, Yekaterinburg, it is best known as the city where the last Tsar and his family were executed by the Bolshevik authorities the year Pavel was born.

Pavel's family had a cow, a dozen pigs, some chickens and ducks.

"So we were *not* rich," says Pavel. Yet the young Party man he punched was only the advance guard for the massive collectivization of agriculture that soon forced his family off the farm and into a near-by town, where Pavel finished primary school and found his first job, in a print shop.

In a personal odyssey that reads like a Siberian Horatio Alger story, Pavel escaped this bleak and unpromising environment to eventually become head of the Russian department at a major United States university, nominee for President of a nonexistent Russian republic, and creator of the longest book in verse ever written in Russian by a single author. The book was published in 1979, thirty-five years after it was begun—a fact which reflects the determination and single-mindedness of its author, as well as the long and tortuous road he traveled from the Ural Mountains to the Kennebec Valley of Maine.

The first step on that road, he says, was a part-time job in Yekaterinburg, where he was a boarding student in high school. "I worked as a typesetter, and studied at night. That job gave me a love for our Russian language and our literature. I read most of the great Russian writers and poets—Pushkin was the greatest influence on me—and I began to write some poetry of my own." Pavel took a second step toward the world beyond his village in 1936, when he entered the Institute of Journalism in Yekaterinburg. Because the Stalin regime needed the support and loyalty of budding journalists, students there received the top stipend of 262 rubles a month, twice that of students in most other fields. Pavel has a photo of his 1940 graduating class. "Five members are missing," he says. "They had already been recruited by the N.K.V.D. (security police), and could not have their names and pictures made public. All the rest, except for one other man and myself, were invited to apply for Communist Party membership. I knew I would not be asked. . . I had never been active in Party affairs—never joined the Young Pioneers or *Komsomolsk* (Party youth organizations). My professors knew how I felt . . . no open rebellion, of course. But they knew, for example, that I liked the pre-Revolutionary Russian writers who were *non*-socialist. That was enough.

"Just before graduation a member of the Party's Central Committee, the editor of *Pravda*, came to the Institute for our final exams. He asked us questions and decided which newspapers we would be assigned to. He told me I would work for an army paper, *Red Star*, in Khabarovsk—the Far Eastern military district—as soon as I came back from vacation. But when I returned, the people at the Institute said, 'Well, the N.K.V.D. refuses to issue you a visa for the Soviet Far East. You're free.' Which meant I had no job. I was the only member of the class not trusted by the Party to work on a newspaper."

Pavel returned home, where the curator of the local museum created a job for him, giving talks and arranging displays. By then the country's mobilization for war had begun. In June 1941, a week before Hitler invaded the U.S.S.R., Pavel was recruited into a labor battalion, tasked with building underground munition storages in the Ural Mountains. "We worked twelve-hour days, seven days a week, with little food," he remembers.

A few months later, following the crushing defeat of Soviet forces and the massive losses of men and material in the first weeks of Hitler's *blitzkrieg*, the Red Army was desperately short of trained men. "The educated men in the labor battalion, including a few like me with college degrees, were put into a separate training platoon. After a month we were sent to Yekaterinburg. When we were marched down the main street, I knew where we were: near an infantry school. I told the men near me, 'If we turn left here, we're going to be trained as infantry officers.'" They turned left, entered a large courtyard, and began four months' officer-training. The war situation was so critical that Stalin was conscripting everyone—especially educated people like Pavel, despite his political unreliability.

In March 1942 Pavel, now a First Lieutenant in the ski troops, was sent to the Finnish front as a platoon leader. It was a strange war among the pine forests and frozen lakes, a war in which Russians and Finns sometimes fraternized in their struggle against the main enemy, the cold. "We and the Finnish troops opposite our lines even built and shared a sauna," Pavel recalls. "And one day one of our political officers walked over to it, not knowing what was going on. Suddenly he saw some naked men with religious crosses hanging around their necks. He rushed up them, yelling 'Take those crosses off immediately!' One of the soldiers—they were all Finns, of course—hit him with his fist. Others pointed their guns at him and said, 'You sit still right there until our men have finished bathing.'"

The war against the Finns did not go well for the Russians. After a year's fighting, Pavel was captured. He had no way of knowing at the time that his capture would be a third and critical event in the break with his past life.

His initial apprehension at being captured quickly gave way to surprise over the casual attitude of his captors. "I asked them, 'Well, why don't you carve a five-pointed star on my forehead and cut off my ears?' That's what we were told they did to Soviet prisoners, although I didn't really believe it. But they didn't even search me before taking me to regional headquarters for interrogation. An officer there said, 'Why don't you sit down?' I said, 'No, not until I remove some of the grenades and ammo I have under my coat.' He said, 'Okay, just put them in the corner over there.' So I pulled out ten grenades and some cartridge clips and piled them on the floor. Then they asked me what I wanted to do. Imagine! I said, 'Aren't you going to put me in a POW camp?' They said, 'Look, we have 250,000 Soviet POWs. That's more men than our whole army has. We can't guard them all, so 100,000 are working on farms.' I told them I was a farmer, but they said, 'Maybe you could do something more intellectual.' They seemed to know a lot about me. They phoned Helsinki, and I understood the words 'journalist' and 'radio' in the conversation. When he rang off he said, 'Okay, you're going to Helsinki. You'll speak on radio.' I asked how they knew so much about me. He laughed and began telling things about my own regiment that I didn't know myself. He told me how they had tapped into our phone lines all along the front."

Guarded by a Finnish noncommissioned officer, Pavel went by train to Helsinki, where he was taken to a summer *dacha* on the city's outskirts. "I was given civilian clothes, and allowed to take long walks in the woods accompanied by a guard. Every evening a man—a Russian born along the Russo-Finnish border in Karelia—came to talk with me. Together we listened to Finnish propaganda broadcasts to the Soviet forces, and he would ask my comments. He also showed me their Russian-language newspaper for POWs, and after a few days I began to write articles for it on what was happening in the U.S.S.R., based on BBC and German broadcasts that I listened to.

"After a couple of weeks the man identified himself as chief of Russian-language broadcasts, and told me I would be working for him. There were seven or eight of us on the staff. We intercepted 'private' news bulletins from a central Soviet information office to regional Soviet newspapers. I would base my next day's broadcasts on those intercepts.

"I worked there almost a year, until the spring of 1944. By then waves of Soviet bombers were attacking Helsinki. In March we were told to 'soften' our propaganda—'don't criticize Stalin too much'—so we understood that some sort of peace negotiations had begun between Finland and the U.S.S.R., and the Finns were preparing to sue for peace. So we were ordered to broadcast pieces about Finland—a visit to a dairy farm, et cetera—and no more anti-Soviet propaganda. The fighting was still going on. So I said, 'well, there's no more work for me here. I'll go to the front and broadcast to my old regiment.' I joined a Finnish Army propaganda unit in Karelia, opposite my old unit. No, I didn't tell them to defect. I urged them to turn their weapons against their officers and seize power."

By then Pavel, who had been working under his given name, Petukhov, had been listed in *Pravda* as a war criminal, he says, sentenced to death in absentia. With Finland's surrender, he was on the Soviet list of those sought for return to the U.S.S.R. for execution. Indeed, Soviet military delegations were already arriving and traveling about in Finland. Pavel therefore changed his name to Vaulin. With the personal help of his boss at the propaganda office he escaped to Sweden in October 1944.

The Swedes issued him an alien's "passport," allowing him to work. During the next five years Pavel took a variety of odd jobs: farmer, woodcutter, newspaper delivery boy, hotel deskclerk, and weaver. In his spare time he resumed work on a book begun in Finland and learned enough Swedish to read about Sweden's history.

In 1950 he joined a group of around a hundred other Russian refugees who hired a Baltic fisherman to take them to America. They were careful to keep their plans secret and to slip away late at night, since an earlier group had been intercepted by a Soviet ship and forced to return to the U.S.S.R.

"Our boat was overloaded," Pavel recalls, "and the fisherman had no charts or compass. But somehow, after fourteen days, we landed in the Azores. We were out of food, almost out of fuel and water. The people there were good to us. They gave us provisions and filled our fuel tank. The Governor's wife herself came down to the dock and brought us food and several cases of wine."

From there the boat set forth again, this time with Boston as its destination. "We approached the United States coast a couple of weeks later in thick fog. We had no radar, not even a fog horn, so I stood up front listening. Suddenly I heard an engine close ahead. As I shouted at the fisherman to go into reverse, I saw this huge side of a ship almost on top of us. Our reverse gear didn't work. The other boat heard my shout and swerved away, but not before hitting us and knocking a big hole just above the water line. They offered to take us aboard. But we stuffed clothing in the hole and told them we would go on." The other boat alerted the Coast Guard. As the fog lifted the refugees saw Cape Cod, and a Coast Guard cutter bearing down on them. "We were afraid they would order us back out to sea. So we killed the engine and told them it had broken down. Another boat came and towed us to Provincetown, and later to Boston. A big article about us, with pictures of our arrival, was published in the *Boston Globe* that day. I remember it was August twenty-ninth, 1950."

Pavel and the others were taken to Ellis Island for processing. "We saw the Statue of Liberty," he recalls with a smile, "but her back was turned toward us." During his five-months' wait for immigration clearance Pavel swept floors in his Ellis Island barracks; he was paid ten cents an hour plus ninety cents a day.

In February 1951 he was cleared to enter the United States as a refugee. With no money, no U.S. friends, and almost no English, Pavel began his life in America close to the bottom economically and professionally. He rented a room in Yonkers, where his first job was washing cars. "After a couple of months I found work at a hospital for $110 a month plus food. I studied English at night school. Then I heard of a job in Tarrytown at something called 'Fisher Body.' I didn't know what sort of place it was, so I appeared there the first day wearing boots and *fishing* clothes!" Recounting these events more than forty years later, Pavel recalls clearly how much each of his early jobs paid. "I stayed several months with General Motors, who paid me $1.73 an hour. Then I got a job with a pipeline company, cutting trees for $2.00 an hour, plus full weekend work at overtime pay."

Meanwhile Pavel had made some Russian acquaintances and attended services at an old Russian Orthodox church in Yonkers. The first was a Christmas service, which he found far different from those he had attended in Europe. "It was a great building constructed in Tsarist times. But it seemed strange to me . . . it had *benches* inside . . . not just a few along the walls for old people, but all over, for *everybody* to use. The priest came out and spoke in English about the need for money. Then the priest, *himself*, took the collection plate around and made sure everyone contributed. Then he disappeared for a long time. When he came out I expected the service to begin. Instead, he announced that the collection came to $173! Only then did he conduct the Christmas service."

Pavel also resumed writing articles for *Rossiya*, a Russian-language journal to which he had contributed during his years in Sweden. He says the journal was considered anti-Semitic, which he did not fault. Nor does he make any attempt to conceal his own extremist worldview, which is informed by a strong Russian nationalism, deep devotion to the Russian Orthodox Church including its more mystical aspects, and more traditional right-wing anti-Semitic conspiracy theories of global events.

Indeed, his understanding of such events is almost identical with that first formalized in the 1905 program of the Union of Russian People. Although its stated purpose was to resist political reform and "preserve intact the monarchy, Russian Orthodoxy, and the Empire"—goals that Pavel would find congenial—at its core stood a vicious anti-Semitism. Jews were seen as "dominating the press, banking, and, through Masonic societies, all spheres of Russian life." Colluding in this alleged global conspiracy were Masons, liberals, capitalists, foreigners—especially Westerners—all of whom were seen as "instruments of the Jews."[1]

It is Pavel's unshakable conviction that a Zionist-orchestrated worldwide conspiracy exists today and was responsible for, among other events, the Bolshevik seizure of power in Russia in 1918. When asked if his ideas were influenced by his wartime experience as an anti-Soviet propagandist, he bridles. "My political ideas have never changed. Not once. Never. Even as a child I knew what was going on in the U.S.S.R."

Pavel recognizes that his extremist political views clash with mainstream Russian immigrant thinking. In late 1951, for example, he introduced himself to the editor of *Novoye Russkoye Slovo*, the oldest and arguably the most mainstream Russian-language newspaper published in the United States. "I had heard that officials of the United States Army Language School (now the Defense Language Institute) in Monterey, California were coming to New York looking for Russian language teachers. I didn't know where interviews were being held, so I asked the editor. He said, 'I know you. I know your writings. You wouldn't fit in at Monterey.' He refused to give me the address. But I found out from his assistant editor and went for an interview. And in January 1953 I was told to report for work in Monterey in thirty days." Pavel believes he was hired because of two friends on the staff who felt the students would benefit by the presence of a recent Soviet immigrant. "The rest of the teachers were old émigrés, who had left Russia before the revolution."

After Pavel had taught there two years, the school underwent a reduction-in-force and he was dropped. He believes his termination was due in part to his vocal objection to the labels on Soviet films used in teaching. "They came with the label 'This film contains no propaganda.' I told my students to scratch that out. All Soviet films had propaganda."

After leaving Monterey Pavel went to Washington, D.C., where he applied for a job with the Voice of America. "Since I was not a United States citizen at that time and had no permanent residence, they could not hire me. So I lived on unemployment insurance and studied English at George Washington University night school, and resumed work on a book I had begun in Finland during the War."

But the interview with Voice of America may have been responsible for a mysterious telephone call Pavel received a few months later which led to his next big job break. "The caller asked me to come for an interview, but was vague about his organization. I was told to go to Room 10, 10th floor, of a building on 10th Street—and he asked me if I thought I could remember the address! The men who interviewed me were from the Pentagon. When I told them I wasn't a United States citizen, they said, 'That's all right. We know a lot about you.' And they did. They had been in contact with Pavel Haupt, my old boss at the Finnish propaganda section. They asked me to sign a secrecy agreement, and would I object to using a false name. I told them I had used several by then. So they hired me to write and tape clandestine radio pieces for broadcast to the U.S.S.R." At that time clandestine United States broadcasts were being transmitted from Taiwan, Norway, and from ships in the Black Sea, all of which were claimed to originate on Soviet territory. "The Soviets made strong efforts to jam them," Pavel says, "but we know they got through. People in the U.S. Embassy heard them." Pavel worked there until the program was closed down in 1959.

By far his most bizarre job opportunity came a year later, when he was called to a secret meeting in Washington, D.C. with U.S. Ambassador Jacob Beam. There, in the company of fellow refugees from other Soviet republics—Uzbekistan, Belorussia, Tajikistan, and others—Pavel heard Ambassador Beam outline a plan to weaken Stalin's hold over the Soviet Union's far-flung empire. "The idea was to promote the breakup of the U.S.S.R.—that is, the territory traditionally making up the old Russian Empire—into smaller states. He offered each of us the *Presidency* of a free democratic republic. He nominated me President of an entity to be called the Idel-Ural Federation!" As a Great Russian nationalist, Pavel was strongly opposed to such a policy. "At the first meeting I asked Ambassador Beam, 'Why split up Russia? Why not split *Communism* from Russia instead?' I listened to him describe the plan. Then I stood up and said, 'I refuse to be a part of this,' and I marched out, slamming the door. As I walked along the hall I heard footsteps behind me. I looked around, and there were the other 'Presidents'—Uzbek, Belorus, Kazakh, Tajik, and others—who had followed me out. Only the Ukrainian and Baltic 'Presidents' remained." Pavel cites this as evidence that the sense of *Rossiyanie*—that is, of belonging to a greater entity embracing Russia and all the constituent parts of the old Russian Empire—remains strong among its various ethnic minorities.

After refusing to serve as President of the nonexistent Idel-Ural Federation, Pavel had to settle for a time doing translations of

Russian-language materials for the U.S. Joint Publications Research Service (better known by its initials, J.P.R.S.). Within another year he had received an M.S. degree in Linguistics from Georgetown University. For his thesis he had written a history of Russian folklore.

Meanwhile, two big changes had occurred in his personal life. In 1958 he had purchased sixty acres of rural land outside Richmond, Maine, and a year later he had met his future wife, Galina, whom he married in 1960. "I bought this land to be near other Russians, people who spoke my native language. There was a hut on it then. But I had future vacations in mind, not permanent residence," he says. Galina is an artist who was living in Boston when they first met to discuss her illustrations for a book he was working on. "We had corresponded before that," she recalls, "but in 1959 he asked to come see me. After we were married, we came to live in Pavel's hut here for awhile, and he began building this (present) house. But he needed a job, so we went to Washington where Pavel studied at night and worked in a print shop during the day. A year later our son, Leo, was born prematurely."

After getting his Master's degree, Pavel was hired to teach Russian language and literature at Boston University. "I taught Russian literature, in English, to eighty undergraduates and to graduate seminars. Then Dr. Merlino, the department chairman, retired; and I became head of the department, which had 249 students." He also gave talks on Russian history, literature, and music over the local public radio station. After three years, however, the University's president told Pavel he would have to have a Ph.D. to be given tenure. So in 1966 he was dropped from the Boston University faculty.

The Vaulins then moved to Mobile, Alabama, where Pavel headed the Russian language and literature department at the University of South Alabama—a position he held until his retirement seventeen years later. "By then," says Galina, "our son Leo had graduated from the University with a degree in computer science. Pavel had wanted him to become a doctor. So Leo started in a premed course to please his father, but didn't like it at all." That was probably not the first time, and certainly not the last, that Leo would have serious qualms about going against the wishes of his stern and strong-minded father.

Meanwhile Galina, who was born into an artistic and intellectual family in the cosmopolitan city of Kiev, found life in Mobile far from stimulating culturally and intellectually. She missed the great museums and galleries of Boston and Washington, as well as the academic ferment of those cities. "The people we met in Mobile were mostly well-to-do landowners, and they just weren't much interested in the arts or world events, or even in education. And in general they were snobbish."

She recalls the first time they visited the prestigious private school attended by their son, who was then fourteen. There is still hurt in her voice as she tells the story fifteen years later. "It was parents' night, with classrooms open and a chance to meet the teachers. But when we arrived Leo was not around, and we knew nobody. Then we walked down a corridor, and Leo came walking toward us with another student. And he walked right by us, without even acknowledging us! He was ashamed of having Russian parents."

Within a few years, however, Leo was no longer embarrassed by his Russian roots. "Pavel had insisted on teaching him Russian every morning for fifteen minutes before he left for school. By the time he was a senior in prep school Leo was getting occasional work translating technical articles from Russian to English. Now, when he calls home, he speaks only Russian."

Pavel and Galina, together with her mother, moved to Richmond following Pavel's retirement in 1984. There they lived until 1997 in the modest, well-designed frame house which he himself had built in 1960. Pavel also excavated two large ponds forming an irregular "L" around the back and one side of the house. "You can usually see our great heron there," he said as he showed a visitor around his property. It was obvious that Pavel enjoyed its fields and woods and semi-isolation two miles from Richmond village.

Most astonishing is a large, solid, one-story building of stone and concrete which Pavel constructed behind the house. The base is of natural fieldstone, the walls above it a mosaic of 10,000 cubes of granite that once paved the streets of Gardiner. "The house isn't finished yet," he said as he unlocked the steel door. "There will be a second floor." The walls, floor, and ceiling are cement. Steel beams encased in cement support the roof. Steel doors separate the several ground-floor rooms, the largest and lightest of which has a fieldstone fireplace and is used as his study. A kitchen and bath have been roughed in, but lack plumbing fixtures.

The basement is another surprise. "The walls are four feet thick," he says. Daylight enters through a series of slanting, tubular windows, like deep portholes, evenly spaced along three sides. A low, circular wall in the center of the floor surrounds the opening of a deep well fed by spring water. One wall has steel rungs built in. "That's an escape hatch," he laughs, "in case you lock yourself in by mistake." When a visitor suggested he name the building *Petropavlovsk*—an old Russian fortress—since it should last 300 years, Pavel grinned. "Yes, I expect it to last *at least* that long." But he rejected the suggestion that he had built it with a nuclear holocaust or Armageddon in mind.

Yet Pavel's chief artistic endeavor—a project that engaged him on and off since his days in Finland during World War II—is a spiritual story, told in verse, with an apocalyptic theme. Called *The Legend of Kitezh* and first published in 1979,[2] it is, says Pavel, the longest book ever written in verse in Russian by a single author. The original legend is both ancient and beautiful. "Kitezh," Pavel explains, "is a mythical city believed to have been situated on the Vietluga River, near the present city of Nizhni Novgorod (roughly 300 miles east of Moscow). In the thirteenth century, during the Tartar invasion, Kitezh was spared for a long time because it was hidden deep in the forest. But a Russian traitor led the Tartars to the city. The people, seeing the Tartars massing for attack, went to their church to pray. God answered their prayers by screening the city in fog. The Tartars waited for the fog to lift. But when it did, Kitezh had disappeared. In its place was Lake Svietloye, which is still there today." Centuries later, says Galina, "people who lived in the village of Voskresenye nearby said that on clear, calm days they could peer into the lake and see cupolas of the old city. And sometimes at night they could hear church bells ringing from the lake." According to the legend, says Pavel, Kitezh and its people were saved by being taken into the holy sphere where they remained invisible.

Part I of his book is about people's lives as lived today. Part II is about life in the holy sphere created by God. "The road to Kitezh," he says in his introduction, "goes into the heavenly sphere of mankind's spirit." While expressing hope that the world will be able to avoid a nuclear catastrophe, he writes that if it should come and our planet is destroyed, "then there ought to be a sanctuary where life can continue." He suggests that the holy sphere in which the invisible town of Kitezh has continued to exist can become that sanctuary where the life of the spirit can go on. The book is beautifully illustrated with Galina's fine pen-and-ink drawings, which appear on every page. A revised edition was published in 1994 in Russia.

While the book attests to Pavel's deep spirituality and devotion to the Orthodox faith, it also places him in what one Church source describes as the mystical outer fringe of Orthodox believers. That fringe, which includes some members of the clergy, lays much emphasis on the apocalyptic passages in the *Book of Revelations*, including the notion of a Second Coming of Jesus and an ultimate war against the "antiChrist." The dark side of Pavel's mysticism is reflected in his deeply held conspiratorial views of world events: an interlocking global network of powerful groups in the service of international Zionism serving as the "antiChrist."

During the early 1980s Pavel published *NIVA (National Institution for a Victorious America)* in both English and Russian. Identified as a quarterly journal of literature and contemporary life, the English edition carried translations from Dostoevsky and others (e.g., an article, "Communism and Morals" by a Dr. Alexander Philipov, otherwise not identified), as well as polemical pieces by Pavel himself. In them he criticized contemporary United States policy for allegedly dividing the Russian people and falling under the influence of "an international mafia of three hundred American and European banking families." In a successor quarterly journal, *The Word*, published since moving to Richmond, Pavel has charged the Federal Reserve, the Trilateral Commission, the Council on Foreign Relations, and other mainstream institutions with "working to create one world Federation and to prepare the world for the coming antiChrist."

Far more original and interesting is his novel, *Notes of a Secret Agent*, privately published and serialized in *The Word* in 1989. In it the hero appears before a newly convened non-Communist Russian legislature and is asked to tell them what kind of Russia he would like to see brought into being. In what appears to be the author's notion of an idealized future Russia, the hero sees "Russia, one and indivisible . . . consisting of three holy entities: God, Tsar, People . . . [in a People's Monarchy] . . .The elected representatives of all the people come together in a Congress and elect the Tsar of Russia [whose word] is the highest law of the land."

Pavel and Galina remained active and contributing members of St. Alexander Nevsky parish church for almost a decade after moving to Richmond. His commitment to the Orthodox Church was practical as well as spiritual: he quietly gave a thousand dollars to a local youth being trained for monkhood at the Orthodox seminary in Jordanville, New York.

Yet Pavel's extremist views, including his anti-Semitism, found little or no support among the other parishioners at St. Alexander Nevsky. While his gentle wife, Galina, has made a number of friends among parish wives, Pavel seems more a loner: a man whose devotion to his writing and whose unconventional political agenda would have prevented his seeking or forming many close friendships with their more conventional husbands.

On at least one occasion the public display of his views became an embarrassment. One of the younger parish women had been asked by Father Chad, the parish priest, to interpret for a group of some twenty visitors, mostly young adults, from Russia. She remembers, "As they were getting on their bus to leave Richmond a local Russian [Vaulin] came up and began to hand out pamphlets printed in Russian. Father Chad's Russian wasn't very good then, and I wasn't paying attention. But as the leaflets were passed out one of the visitors shouted in Russian, 'Hey, these are anti-Semitic!' So I looked at one, and when I saw that they were these right-wing political tracts, I tore them out of the hands of these startled visitors. I don't know what they must have thought."

In 1992 Pavel visited the former U.S.S.R. for the first time since leaving fifty years before. He went mainly to explore the possibilities of publishing his book there. "I also wanted to see with my own eyes what's going on there. It was almost like a new country to me. The city centers looked about the same. But the suburbs and outlying areas were all new; and there were so many *younger* people everywhere."

No longer apprehensive over the possibility of being jailed for his wartime activities, Pavel used his original family name, Petukhov, in booking internal flights. "The local authorities where I had lived knew my background. You see, there weren't that many Russian emigrants to America from the Urals region. So my visit was written up in the local papers, and I was invited to give talks about my life in America. But the authorities no longer cared about my past."

Pavel also visited his two brothers living in the area, neither of whom he had seen since leaving for the Front in 1941. His trip to post-Soviet Russia seemed to kindle, for a time at least, thoughts of returning to his old homeland to live; he has close relatives living there and believes that his U.S. pension would go much further in Russia.

Meanwhile Pavel, and more particularly Galina, were tied down by the presence of her ninety-year-old mother, who had been ill and bedridden for several years. This virtually ruled out any social life for the Vaulins. Even Galina's attendance at St. Alexander Nevsky Church services offered little relief, since she had to skip the coffee hour afterward in order to go home and care for her mother. Like many in the Russian-speaking colony, however, Galina refused even to consider placing her mother in a nursing home. Pavel supported her in this. In 1994 her mother died. Shortly thereafter, apparently in reaction to the shock of losing her after so many years, Galina suffered a mild heart attack.

In 1995 the calm routine of their lives was again disrupted by a family event—a particularly happy one for Galina: their son Leo's disclosure that he had married a local woman in Alabama several years before, and that they had a son, given the Russian name Román, who was two years old. Leo had delayed telling his parents about either event, Galina says, because of his father's strong and long-declared intention that Leo should marry a Russian Orthodox woman, preferably a Siberian. Galina first learned of her daughter-in-law and grandson during a visit to Alabama to see Leo. She, too, found it difficult to tell Pavel, however. She finally broke the news to him at Boston's Logan Airport as he was about to leave for a second visit to Siberia. Since then she has taken growing delight in her grandson, whom she has come to know now that she is free to travel.

Initially, however, Pavel reacted to the news of an American daughter-in-law and grandson with studied ambivalence. He shrugged off a friend's congratulations saying, "How can my grandson be brought up in the [Orthodox] faith? Who will instruct him?"

In the spring of 1996, however, the Vaulins' son Leo brought three-year-old Román for a visit. During their stay Román was baptized into the Russian Orthodox faith, for which Pavel gave thanks to God.

In 1997 the Vaulins moved to Jordanville, New York, to be near the Orthodox seminary there.

CHAPTER FIVE

COSSACK INTERLUDE:
LARA'S STORY

IVAN SITCHENKO, THE LAST *ATAMAN* of Kennebec Valley's aging Don Cossack veterans, died in 1988 at age 100. As a professional soldier serving in the Tsar's Cossack regiment he won his Sergeant's stripes fighting the Germans in the First World War. When Russia's civil war broke out a few years later he became an officer in General Denikin's "White" (i.e., anti-Communist) Army, and fought to defend his Don Valley homeland against the fledgling Red Army. After the collapse of Denikin's forces, Sitchenko fled Russia, emigrating to the United States in 1923. Other Cossacks settled in Yugoslavia, where they later organized a Cossack Regiment, hoping to fight the Soviets in World War II.

The death of Sitchenko, the *ataman* or honorary headman, marked the formal end of Cossack activities in Maine. In fact the local Cossack council, the *stanitsa*, of which he had been *ataman* since coming to Maine in 1953, had shrunk from 100 members at that time to twenty-five by 1968, when they held what was to become the last official Cossack reunion in the state. As described in the *Maine Sunday Telegram* of 24 November 1968:

Shot glasses filled with vodka clinked in the pine-panelled

Sportsman's Club outside Richmond as Maine's remaining Cossacks—émigrés of a half century ago who escaped the Bolshevik terror of 1919—got together. At the end of six rounds of toasts, hearty Cossack songs rang out over the rolling fields and skeet shooting range of the small frame clubhouse perched on a knoll.

Tanya Petrochenko, who lived with Sitchenko for thirty-five years, remembered their active social life in the 1950s and 1960s. As the *ataman's* de facto wife, Tanya, who was twenty years younger than her husband, arranged and took an active part in the *stanitsa's* celebrations. "We bought a house on the Sheepscot in Dresden, fixed it up, and did a lot of entertaining there, especially for the big Cossack celebrations." She spoke in particular about the *pokrová*—an annual Orthodox ceremony going back to the sixteenth century when the Virgin Mary is believed to have descended to place a cloak of fog over a Cossack force, enabling it to escape annihilation by a Muslim army. Group photographs of that celebration show local Cossacks and their wives, together with the Orthodox priest and visiting dignitaries, gathered around a banquet table. Sitchenko, tall, straight, and handsome with a short military mustache, could pass for Hollywood's version of a lean British Army general. In the background are the American flag and Cossack regimental flags. A painting of the Virgin holding the miraculous cloak is prominently displayed.

But by no means all the settlers of Cossack descent took an active part in the *stanitsa's* activities, even at their height in the 1960s. Pyotr Razko, who was in his forties at the time, recalls that his Cossack father was totally uninterested. "He called it 'children's games.' It was mostly a few old men, and when the *ataman* died, that was the end of it. A few of our families did get together for holidays, mostly food and drink and singing in our homes. And of course *all* the families in the *stanitsa*—the local Cossack community—attended the Orthodox service celebrating *pokrová* every October. We still do." The local Cossacks of Pyotr's generation, however, were too busy working and raising young families to spend time in meetings of the *stanitsa's* old veterans. Few of them knew or much cared what went on there.

Pyotr and Lara Razko are typical of this group. Both were born in the U.S.S.R. into Cossack families of the Don region. In Richmond their fathers, retired by then, found company and comfort among the *stanitsa's* other venerable warriors. Meanwhile Pyotr and Lara ran a small farm on the bank of the Kennebec, took care of their aging parents at home, raised a large family, and commuted to jobs at Bath Iron Works twenty miles away.

While adapting to an American lifestyle like that of many native-born Mainers, the Razkos seem to have led a more isolated existence than most. Their social lives revolve almost exclusively around children and grandchildren, and a couple of Russian friends. In part this stems from their location—Richmond, the nearest town, is seven miles away—and the heavy demands of work and family. But their non-involvement with people and organizations in the broader community, even though both Lara and Pyotr speak English well, also appears to be in part self-imposed: a result of their youth spent under Soviet rule, and the caution it engendered toward involvement with authority and with outsiders.

They agreed to be interviewed, for example, only if their real names not be used. Pyotr, in particular, seemed reluctant to talk about his activities under the German occupation. "People here [in America] don't understand what it was like for people like us in World War II," he says. "We were just tossed back and forth," and he swings his arm violently to illustrate. Both Pyotr and Lara express fears that some of the things that happened, some of the decisions they or their parents made in those years, might be taken out of the context of chaos and violence, of having little or no control over their own young lives, and might be misunderstood. And they fear that, even after all these years, such a misunderstanding might somehow adversely affect the careers of their five children, two of whom are career officers in the U.S. armed forces.

The Razkos are proud of their children, all of whom were born in America. They are proud, too, that two of them are carrying on the Cossack tradition of military service to their country. Pride in their Cossack roots also emerges in their stories, tinged with a still-smoldering bitterness over Stalin's treatment of the Cossack people, and over an appalling incident toward the end of World War II in a British Army-run camp for Cossack Displaced Persons (DPs) when the British protectors suddenly turned their weapons on the unarmed Cossacks—an event burned deep in the memories of Lara and Pyotr, who witnessed the attack.

Lara was born in the city of Rostov, where the Don flows into the sea. Her father was a soldier, trained as a medical specialist. "He joined General Denikin's White Forces during the civil war. He later told me that when the Reds under Voroshilov pushed them to the Black Sea, he had one of two choices: either jump into the sea or join Voroshilov. So he tore the colored stripes from his trousers, threw away his army cap, and suddenly reappeared as a volunteer recruit to serve in the new Red Army."

Lara's most vivid memory of early childhood occurred during what she and Pyotr call the "Great Hunger" along the Don steppe. It was the period when Stalin's ruthless drive to industrialize the U.S.S.R. and collectivize the farmers was carried out through forced seizures of grain for export and total disruption of traditional agriculture, resulting in the deaths of millions. "It was the very early 1930s. There were huge piles of grain rotting by the roadside, grass growing out of them. And people were starving. One winter day in town my mother suddenly reached down and covered my head so I would not see a truck that was passing by. But I peeked out. The truck was loaded with the bodies of people who had frozen to death . . . I saw their legs sticking out of the back of the truck, like sticks of wood."

Both Lara and Pyotr attribute the "Great Hunger" to a conscious campaign by Stalin to turn the people against each other, thereby weakening his political opposition. They believe that the Cossack people were treated particularly harshly because of their centuries-old tradition of militancy and rebellion against governmental authority. Two of the bloodiest revolts in Russia's history were organized and led by Cossacks: Stenka Razin's rebellion in 1667 and Yemelyan Pugachev's a century later. "So Stalin didn't trust the Cossacks," says Lara. "He broke up their traditional organization, the *stanitsa*, which was a sort of village council headed by an elected *ataman*, who was also its military leader. And he took away all their riding horses—took them away from the people who for centuries have been famous as the horsemen of the steppe! It was the Cossack cavalry who defended Cossack lands from invaders. So taking away his horse strikes at the heart of what it means to be a Cossack." Lara speaks with a touch of bitterness about some members of Richmond's "First Wave" Russian immigrants. "Some of them looked down on us, the 'Second Wave,' and said we were Communists since we had lived in the U.S.S.R. during the 1930s. They didn't know how badly Stalin treated the Cossacks. We had no love for Stalin."

Lara recalls incidents of the intrusiveness and suspicions of Soviet authorities. "During the Hunger another Cossack woman, much older than me, had one of those traditional wide Caucasian belts decorated with inserts of silver. It was her prized possession. But they needed money. So she removed the little strips of silver from the belt and turned them in at the local State Bank in exchange for currency. A few days later she was called in to the local office of the N.K.V.D.—the security police—and was held there for a week and questioned, because they suspected her of hoarding silver."

During this period Lara's father worked at odd jobs while attending medical school. "But by the time he completed his studies in 1934 he was already forty-four years old—too old to consider going on to specialize. So he joined the Anti-Plague Institute in Rostov, and was soon appointed as its director. He was responsible for administering several plague clinics in the Kalmyshnii steppe, an area that was subject to the bubonic plague spread by the local prairie-dog population.

"I had always been interested in my father's lab work . . . he called me his *sulfereek*—a person with strong curiosity. But of course I couldn't work in his plague lab, where security was very strict. I went to school in Rostov, and completed seven years before World War II came. The first real event of the war in our area was a tremendous explosion, when a secret Soviet ammunition dump in the outskirts of the city blew up. After that my father moved us to a village far away from Rostov.

"As the Germans approached our village in late 1941, my father and his staff destroyed all the bubonic plague virus in the lab so it would not fall into German hands. Then he closed the lab and went to a nearby Kalmyk village, quite a primitive settlement, where the

Kalmyk people hid him until he was sure he could return home without being interned by the Germans. As he left our village he handed me the keys to the Institute's compound, and told me to turn them over to the German commandant as soon as the German troops arrived, and to be sure to tell them that the compound was safe—no plague virus around, no booby-traps around—so that they wouldn't blow it up. I was only fourteen or fifteen at the time, so I asked a friend to go with me. As we walked by the Institute we noticed that German soldiers had been stationed outside the compound, but none were inside. We found the Germans' headquarters, and I turned over the keys to a Russian-speaking officer. He didn't believe me that the Institute was safe. 'If you don't believe me,' I told him, 'I'll walk through the complex and you can follow me.' He did, and later seemed ashamed of being afraid. My father returned a few days later and was questioned by the Germans. He confirmed what I had told them. 'Why wouldn't you believe *her?*' he asked. 'She's only a fourteen-year-old kid, and she was brought up to respect adults and to tell the truth.'"

Within a few months the Germans ordered Lara and her parents to Berlin. They traveled in cattle cars, along with other local families. "The train stopped all along the way to pick up other people. By the time it reached Berlin six weeks later our car was packed tight. We made a small place for ourselves in one corner. The train stopped once or twice a day, and there would be something like a soup kitchen by the tracks where food would be ladled out to us."

In Berlin Lara's father worked in a disease laboratory where research was carried out to seek cures for common childhood diseases, including diphtheria, measles, scarlet fever, and dysentery. Because her father was a professional man whose skills were needed by the Germans, Lara says, the family was not placed in a labor camp, nor forced to wear the hateful "OST" patches identifying "Eastern Workers"—i.e., forced labor from the occupied Slavic countries. Nor had her father been "political," or even a member of the Communist Party in the U.S.S.R. Their Cossack identity may also have been a factor in their favorable treatment, since the Nazis had a long-standing respect for the Cossacks' historical reputation as fierce fighters.[1] In any event, the Cossacks somehow avoided the label of *"untermenschen,"* lower-order human beings, which Hitler applied to other Slavs.

"We were housed in an apartment building with many other Cossack families," says Lara. "And we were free to walk about the city." She recalls the bombing. "At first it happened so seldom, we would go to see what a bombed-out house looked like. Later we would look with curiosity when we saw a house that had *not* been bombed.

"My father got me permission to work in his lab, even though I was only fifteen or sixteen at the time and had no formal scientific training. They were short of personnel, since almost all German doctors were serving with the military. I had learned quite a bit about lab work from my father over the years, and knew what some of the equipment was for. But I had to learn to use a pipette tube correctly to avoid sucking fluids into my mouth, since they all contained disease germs.

"Later, after I got tired of sucking pipette tubes, I got a job for three months as an interpreter for General Krasnov at the Berlin headquarters of the Cossack forces. All three of the Cossack armies fighting the Bolsheviks were represented there." Lara recalls little of this period, although she remembers the Cossack commander as a fine man. "In the final weeks of the war, as Soviet troops were closing in on Berlin, our family escaped thanks to General Krasnov. Without obtaining approval from the German High Command, he organized a train of fifty cars and arranged to empty out all the camps of Russian-speaking people in the Berlin area. The train took us to Tolmezzo, in northern Italy. Italy was out of the war by then."

The several thousand Cossack families encamped there, however, quickly discovered that they had not escaped the war, as Italian partisan guerrillas began attacking their camps. Cossack males, including young Pyotr, fought to defend themselves. Moreover the Allied advance was moving rapidly into northern Italy in the spring of 1945, forcing the German Wehrmacht to retreat. As the Germans prepared to leave, they arranged to evacuate the entire Cossack population across the Alps and into Austria, where they finally would be out of the war. There was no transportation for them. "We were part of a huge column, miles long," Lara remembers. "Some were on horseback, but most were on foot. My father and mother and I walked. After the sunny valley where we had been staying in Italy, we found ourselves tramping through deep snow in the Alps. It was five or six days' walk. Our shoes wore out, so we cut strips from blankets and wound them around our feet. The march was guarded by mounted Cossack units, who kept it orderly. The German Army had provided food for us along the way. One night we stayed in a Catholic monastery. When we finally came down into Austria, our feet were swollen to twice their normal size."

The Cossacks' destination was a British-run camp near the Austrian city of Lienz. There the Cossacks, military and civilian alike, believed that they and their families had reached a safe Western sanctuary, beyond the reach of the Soviets. And it was there they learned the terrible price many of them would pay for the role played by those Cossacks who had served under the Germans in the war.

For Lara and Pyotr, who did not know each other then, their presence at what they call "the betrayal of the Cossacks" would later become a shared experience in terror. Fifty years afterwards their normally calm voices grow shrill and intensely emotional in talking about that event. Pyotr slips into staccato Russian as he relives the shock and anger over what happened.

"We believed the British when their General said they would protect us . . . we weren't prisoners, he said, and we would be free to come and go from the camp. But we had to surrender our guns. That was okay. Then we began hearing rumors about people in other camps being forced to go back to the U.S.S.R." Suspicions were heightened on May twenty-eighth, when the camp's 2,000 Cossack officers failed to return from a meeting they had been asked to attend, supposedly with the commander of the British Eighth Army. In fact, the buses that took them out of the camp were soon joined by a heavily armed British convoy, which delivered them to a Red Army base in the Soviet Zone of Austria. There they were arrested, interrogated, and sent to the U.S.S.R. for trial as war criminals. Senior officers were executed, and the rest sentenced to prison terms in Siberian labor camps.[2]

None of this was known, of course, to the Cossacks waiting in the camp in Lienz. Some, particularly men with no families, left the camp, preferring to try making their way farther west, melting in with the hoards of refugees going the same way. But the vast majority of the camp's roughly 20,000 Cossacks stayed on.

Early in the morning of June first, Lara says, everyone gathered together for the open-air Orthodox mass, as usual. "While we were at mass, we suddenly heard shouting and scuffling at the back of the crowd. British soldiers had come up behind the crowd and were dragging people off—women, children, men . . . anybody—and forcing them into trucks waiting nearby. There was no announcement, no notice, no explanation . . . people were screaming, trying to grab family members and escape . . . it was total chaos. There was shooting . . . I saw an old man the soldiers had shot . . . his guts were spilling out."

Those who escaped being thrown into the trucks ran back through the camp, which was divided by the Isel River. "People were so terrified . . . some parents threw their small children in the river and jumped in after them," Pyotr recalls. "But most of the people kept on running," says Lara, "and scattered into the mountains close by. My father and mother and I just grabbed what clothing we could as we passed the tents where we lived, and ran to hide in the mountains. We could hear truck motors and noise from the main camp; but it died out by evening. No one was left there by then. And of course no one who fled returned there.

"We slept in the woods, away from other people. After a few days we found our way to another DP camp. The people there had not even heard what happened at Lienz. And we never heard anything public about it . . . no explanation, nothing." Lara and her parents stayed on at the second camp until the repatriation issue had quieted down and ex-Soviet DPs were no longer being forced to return to the U.S.S.R. Lara credits this change, at least on the part of the British, with an action taken by the Orthodox priest at Lienz shortly before the June episode. "He had written a letter to King George, asking him to intervene with the British government in behalf of the Cossacks . . . Tsar Nicholas had, after all, been King George's cousin. The priest's letter didn't get there in time to prevent the British betrayal of our people at Lienz. But there were no more incidents after that, so we think the King was responsible for the change."

Lara and Pyotr, like many other former Russian DPs, remain bitter about the failure of the Western wartime leaders, particularly Churchill and Roosevelt, to prevent the forcible repatriation of their countrymen to the U.S.S.R. in the closing months of the war. Caught up in their own struggle for survival, and believing that the West shared their deep hatred of Stalin's regime, many were out of touch with Western attitudes at that time. They were thus unaware of either the degree of Western contempt for anyone who had served under the Nazis, or the strong respect in the West in those pre-Cold War days for the Soviet allies, who had borne so large a part of the burden of defeating Hitler's armies. Many of the Cossack leaders, like their brothers-in-arms in the *Russkii Corpus*, held strong hopes that the Western Allies would follow up the surrender of Nazi Germany with an assault on the U.S.S.R., which lay weakened and exhausted by the war. They were therefore unprepared to be treated as enemies by the West, let alone to become the target of brutal actions like that carried out against the Cossack people in Lienz.

After spending seven years in Austrian DP camps, Lara and her parents won permission to immigrate to the United States in 1952. They settled in New Jersey, where all three found a series of factory jobs. She met Pyotr for the first time at a Cossack social event, and they were married in 1956. Two years later they visited a friend in Richmond who had been extolling the virtues of life in Maine.

"By then," Lara recalls, "we were tired of New Jersey. The streets in Paterson and other cities we had lived in were so dirty. We had a baby daughter who was so unfamiliar with nature, she began to cry in alarm one day when we were in a park and put her down to crawl on the grass. So we took $100 along—our entire savings—when we went to Richmond, and we hoped to find a house and some land where we could raise a family where it was clean and where the air was fresh.

"But it was Memorial Day weekend, cold and rainy, when we got here. It was thick fog. And I *hated* the place. I was ready to go home. But we stayed overnight with our friends. And when we woke up the next morning, the sun was shining, birds were singing . . . it was *beautiful!*"

"So," says Pyotr, "we found *this* house and forty acres. It was in very bad shape, not like you see it today. We put down $50 on it—half our savings. A dumb thing to do, no? We had a baby daughter, we had no jobs here. But we moved here anyway a few months later. We got jobs in local plants right away. And a year after that both sets of parents decided to retire and move up here."

Over the next decade Lara bore four more children. All five children were educated locally and went on to technical school or college. In the summer all of them helped with the haying and with a large vegetable garden, which Pyotr now takes care of by himself. Lara divides her time between her flower garden, which supplies a vast array of potted and hanging plants around the house, and baby-sitting the three grandchildren whose parents live nearby. "And another grandchild is on the way," she says happily.

The neat, attractive house and the quietly busy lives being lived there have clearly served as a happy sanctuary from the stress and violence of Lara's and Pyotr's years in war-torn Europe. Their memories of those early years seem to be buried deep, and to come only rarely to the surface.

One such recurrence happened a few years ago, when the Razkos visited their son who was on U.S. Army duty in Germany. "He was going on a trip to Austria," says Lara. "So we asked him to stop and visit the Cossack cemetery in Lienz. When he asked why we were interested, we told him the whole story. He said, 'Why have you never told me about this before now?' We couldn't really give him an answer. Anyway, he went there with some friends of his. He sent us pictures of the Cossack memorial, with its inscription about Cossacks giving their lives for the liberation of their homeland. A huge cross rises above it. He laid some flowers there, and he and his friends drank a toast in cognac to the Cossacks."

CHAPTER SIX

LIFE AMONG THE CLAN:
BASILIO'S STORY

BASILIO LEPUSCHENKO IS A VIGOROUS MAN of 5'9" with light blue eyes, a shock of white hair, and the ruddy complexion of one who has spent much of his life outdoors. His athletic build and rugged good looks make him appear younger than his sixty-eight years.

Basilio and his wife Natalya live on five acres in the countryside near Richmond in an attractive ranch-style house which he himself built. Behind the house, woods and fields slope gently to the Kennebec a mile away. Their daughter Anna, together with her husband and young daughter, live on an adjoining property in a home Basilio built for them when Anna married. Since both Anna and her husband work during the day, eight-year-old Riana spends after-school hours with her "Baba" Natalya, who also teaches her Russian.

Unlike Pavel Vaulin, a near neighbor for many years, Basilio has lived within a large extended family throughout his almost four decades in America. When his eighty-seven-year-old father, Konrad, died in Richmond in 1988, the local paper noted that: "He is survived by a son, Basilio, three daughters—Natrona, Anna, and Nina—16 grandchildren, and eight great-grandchildren."[1]

For more than twenty years, while their children were growing up, Basilio and his wife owned and worked a farm not far from their present home. The four nearest farms belonged to other family members: Basilio's father and three married sisters. The neighborhood seemed so dense with Lepuschenkos that local Russian people jokingly called the road *Konradovka*—Konradville—after the head of the Lepuschenko clan.

Such close family ties were particularly important during the 1950s, when various relatives began arriving in America with little or no capital and no knowledge of the language, customs, or institutions in the new homeland. Basilio and his father were experienced farmers and carpenters, and were therefore able to help each other, and newly arrived relatives, build houses and barns and get started in chicken-farming. Loans of money within the clan were important in raising small amounts of capital for struggling new ventures in farming and other small-scale enterprise.

This close reliance on the clan did not prevent the Lepuschenkos from rapid assimilation into the culture of their adoptive country. Two of Basilio's three sisters and both of his daughters married non-Russians. All three of his children, including a son born in 1968, earned degrees from American colleges and hold professional jobs. While both Basilio and Natalya have been active members of the Russian-speaking community and the local Orthodox Church, Basilio's growing skills as a cabinet maker and inventor increasingly involved him in business well beyond ethnic and state borders. It has also brought financial security.

Security of any sort was a long time in coming to the Lepuschenkos. Basilio was born in 1926 in a small village in the Belorussian region of the former U.S.S.R. Today it is the independent state of Belarus, established in 1991 after the breakup of the Soviet Union. Because of its location on the U.S.S.R.'s western frontier, Belorussia was quickly overrun by the Nazi *blitzkrieg* in the summer of 1941. It then became the scene of bitter fighting between the occupying Germans and local partisan guerrillas. "We did not join the partisans," says Basilio, "but we were afraid the Germans suspected us of supporting them." Knowing what fearful reprisals were being taken against any such suspects, the Lepuschenkos—Basilio, together with his father, mother, and three sisters—left their home and took refuge in a nearby village. "A few months later the Germans burned our home village and shot all the males found there, including my four uncles and five cousins."

In 1943 heavy fighting see-sawed across Belorussia as the Soviet counteroffensive began. "I was seventeen at the time. I remember seeing the sky in the east lit up by flames." As the war seemed about to engulf them, the family decided to go to the relative safety of Brest-Litovsk, a city near the Polish border. There, however, they and other families in flight were rounded up by the Germans and placed in a so-called "transit camp" nearby, dreading but not knowing where they would be sent next. Basilio escaped. Making his way to Brest-Litovsk, he quickly found work at the city post office, thereby acquiring a most valuable document: a work permit.

"I sneaked back into the camp and passed the work permit to my father. When he showed it to the camp authorities, they allowed all of us to leave. We then found a family who let us stay with them temporarily." Soon they learned that, as the Soviet army advanced, all males who had been in Belorussia during the German occupation were being rounded up and forced into "death battalions," so named because they were sent to the Front, one rifle to every three men, to draw German fire. "I met a survivor from one of those battalions. He had escaped by pretending to be dead and later surrendering to the Germans."

Hearing this and other alarming accounts of Soviet actions as the Red Army advanced, the Lepuschenkos decided to head farther West. In July 1944, when the Germans opened the Polish border to civilian travel, the family boarded a freight car on a west-bound train. That night armed guards were put on the train, which "was shunted around Czechoslovakia for the next two weeks. Our final stop was the town of Dachau. All the people left the cars and walked to a processing camp. There we were lined up and inspected by officials wearing white medical uniforms. People who were too old or too sick to work were separated out and sent to the Dachau concentration camp. We knew it was not a labor camp, but we didn't know then what went on there. Two days later we were marched back to the station. We saw boxcars lined up with destinations painted on their sides—'Innsbruck,' 'Salzburg' and 'Munich.'" The Lepuschenkos, together with 111 other Belorussians, were herded into cars going to

Innsbruck. "That train, we noticed, had no armed guards. It took us to a labor camp at Matrei am Brenner, near the Brenner Pass. The camp was run by German railway personnel, not the army. And the barbed wire had been removed. We were made to sew labels printed with 'OST'—for *Ost Arbeiter,* Eastern Worker—on our clothes. We were free to walk outside the camp on Sundays, but anyone found more than four kilometers away would be sent to concentration camp."

When U.S. forces liberated the area in 1945 the Lepuschenko family and 12,000 other "Eastern Workers" were sent to a Displaced Persons camp near Kufstein, Austria, run by the Americans and later by the French. The Belorussians, like other ethnic groups, were allowed to stay together. They were distraught, however, to learn that the Allied plan was to repatriate all former Soviet citizens to the U.S.S.R., as specified in the Yalta accord. The sole exceptions were those who could prove they had been citizens of Poland or the Baltic states before 1939.

Basilio recalls camp visits by officials from the U.S.S.R. and from U.N.R.R.A., the United Nations Relief and Rehabilitation Agency, to arrange repatriation of Displaced Persons. By then recent escapees from the U.S.S.R. had brought alarming news about Soviet treatment of returnees from German-occupied areas: some older men had been sent to Siberia, and the younger ones forced into labor battalions. Like most of the other Displaced Persons in their camp, the Lepuschenkos were determined to resist repatriation, forcibly if necessary. "So one day I was called before a panel of U.N.R.R.A. officials who asked me if I was ready to go back to the U.S.S.R. I shouted, 'No! I am an anti-Communist.'"

Basilio immediately knew it was a dangerous thing to blurt out, since in the end he might be forced to return anyway. But, after weeks of uncertainty, he and the other Belorussians found that their names had been removed from the repatriation list. Basilio credits their escape to intervention by the wartime Polish Government-in-Exile in London. "The Poles remembered that many Belorussians had served with Polish units fighting on the Allied side in Italy." By then, too, the Western Allies had learned of Soviet treatment of returnees, and were accordingly far more accommodating toward ex-

Soviet citizens who did not want to go back. The Displaced Persons, themselves, were pursuing their own ways of avoiding repatriation. A lively trade in forged passports and birth certificates went on in the DP camps. Pyotr Razko, a Richmond resident and former DP himself, recalls with a laugh the "thousands of people in our camp who spoke nothing but Russian among themselves all day long, but claimed to be Poles or Czechs or Balts."

The Lepuschenkos continued to live in their Austrian DP camp for several years while applying for immigration permits to the West. Basilio and his future wife, Natalya, met in the camp and were married in 1948. That same year her father and other blood relatives emigrated to Argentina, followed two years later by Natalya and Basilio.

He quickly learned Spanish, which he found easier than German and Polish, in which he was already fluent. He worked as a carpenter, and in a few years was part-owner of a home construction company. Later he became building supervisor for a large firm that constructed high-rise apartments and office buildings.

There were still occasional reminders of the nightmare wartime years. "One day I walked into a small clothing shop in La Plata. The owner looked familiar. I said 'I've known you somewhere.' So we began talking about where we had been during the war. He was a Hungarian Jew who had survived several concentration camps. Then suddenly I remembered. When I'd been on a train taking our family to a labor camp, at one of the stops a train was stopped on the other track. We had talked with the people on that train, and I'd tried to buy that man's coat. When I reminded him of that he started to cry. His wife had been killed in one of the camps, and he was the only survivor in his family. I bought a pair of pants. But when I unwrapped the package at home, I found *two* pairs."

Shortly after arriving in Argentina Basilio applied for a United States visa. "In 1957 my number came up. By then we had two small daughters—Irene born in 1951, and Anna born in 1955. At first I felt, 'No, now I don't want to go.' Then the company wanted to send me to work in Rosario, 250 miles away, to oversee a big construction project. Natalya didn't want to leave La Plata. There were other reasons to leave . . . economic problems in Argentina, my wish to be reunited with my family. So we decided to go. Besides, U.S. immigration under President Eisenhower made it easier for relatives overseas to join family members who had already emigrated. So, when we came to America in 1958, my wife's father and brother came with us under the same quota."

Basilio's parents and siblings—two sisters, plus a younger brother born in the DP camp—had already emigrated to America in 1950. His father initially worked on a farm in New York state, but soon carved out a more lucrative career as a carpenter in Rhode Island. In 1954, after reading one of Poushental's advertisements about the Kennebec Valley being like the land they had left back home in Belorussia, they bought a farm and settled in Richmond. "Von Poushental had offered it to him for $4,000. But my father found the actual owner, and bought it for $1,800. He thought he was getting only a fifty-acre farm, but it turned out to be around a hundred."

After bringing his own family to Richmond, Basilio found that his very limited knowledge of English restricted his job opportunities as a skilled carpenter and mason. So he helped his father run a chicken farm and, like many other Russian-speakers in the area, got a job at the local Etonic Shoe factory. "The farm was in debt, so my father accepted an offer from a poultry-processing firm: they supplied the feed and chicks, and paid him $150 a week to raise them. I helped him build a big chicken barn that could handle 45,000 chickens. That raised his income from the processing firm to $450 a week."

Basilio also took immediate steps to master English. " I went to a thirty hours' concentrated course in 'English for Citizenship,' and began reading newspapers, even though I didn't understand much of what I read at first. After passing the citizenship exam, I remember the judge saying 'Congratulations. Now you have the right to wash the dishes.'" But Basilio's feelings resonated more with the positive message given the new citizens by a Czech-American, who instead stressed the opportunities available to them in their new homeland.

Even while working for the low wages of a shoe factory, Basilio had his mind set on ways to achieve financial security for his family. Gradually he acquired the tools needed to expand a small private business building custom kitchen cabinets and remodeling houses. In 1969 he quit the shoe factory job to devote all of his time to cabinet-making and construction.

In the meantime he had bought eleven acres near his father's farm and had built a house there for his wife and two daughters. "I built that first house with used lumber: heavy 6 x 6 posts, some of them thirty feet long, and wide planking, all of which I bought for $200." After a son, Walter, was born in 1968, Basilio borrowed $2,000 from his brother to buy another thirty acres a half-mile away where he built a new house, later selling the first one.

Meanwhile Basilio has carved out a unique professional niche as a builder of Russian stoves, based on his own designs and copyrighted in 1978. A brick structure roughly six feet wide and six feet high, its radiant heat can warm a medium-sized house for an entire Maine winter using only two to three cords of wood. The oil crisis in the early 1970s led to increased demand, which was further spurred by an illustrated article in *Yankee Magazine*, and feature pieces appearing in *Shelter Magazine, Country Living,* and *Mother Earth.*[2] In addition to publishing a how-to manual on his stoves and holding a workshop on their construction, Basilio personally built more than thirty of them throughout Maine. Basilio's work and skills are clearly a source of deep personal pleasure and pride. Although he has high blood pressure and is beyond the age when most people retire, he appears to be a man whose work means far too much to him to give it up. He and his wife are active members of the St. Alexander Nevsky Church, to which he donated his skills and time to build an annex. He served as the Church treasurer and auditor for many years, and is known for his diligence and probity in that office. He is known and respected in the wider Richmond community as well, and was invited to be a member of the town Planning Board—a post which he filled for three years.

Basilio also takes great pride and satisfaction in his family. He is particularly pleased that all three children speak Russian, observe traditional Orthodox holidays, and are proud of their ethnic heritage. His wife Natalya, together with their son and daughters, play traditional Russian instruments and have performed at folk festivals and other events throughout Maine.

But Basilio seems equally pleased by his family's successful integration into the broad American mainstream. Relaxing in a screened gazebo set among a grove of tall sugar maples at the edge of his property, he talked about his life in America with an air of true contentment. "Yes, I am pleased with my family, and with the many friends, both Russian and non-Russian, we have made here," he says. He and a visitor sit quietly, listening to the rustle of maple leaves stirred by the warm summer breeze. Through the trees the handsome split-level house, quintessentially American except for its Russian stove, is barely visible. Natalya calls, and their granddaughter, who has been hovering outside the gazebo listening to her grandfather talk, quietly disappears. The terrors and uncertainties of Basilio's youth in war-torn Eastern Europe remain a clear but distant memory, eclipsed by the past forty years of peace and security in his adoptive homeland.

*   *   *   *   *

In January 1998 Basilio died of cancer. A few months later his eight-year-old granddaughter, Riana, received an A-plus for a science project demonstrating that her grandfather's Russian stove burned more efficiently than traditional American models.

PART THREE

I believe my abiding interest in the development of a professional career came from my father. Sadly I realize how little I really know about him or his earlier life. It seems like he came from another world, another era. He's been gone for thirty-five years, but of course we always carry the parent inside us.

–Day Kokarev Jr., March 1995 letter

CHAPTER SEVEN

THE MAKING OF A UKRAINIAN NATIONALIST:
NICK'S STORY

MAINE'S OFFICE OF HIGHWAY DESIGN seems an unlikely place to find a dedicated Ukrainian nationalist, the scion of an illustrious Ukrainian family whose men rose to eminence in the Russian Navy under three Tsars beginning in the 1850s. Nor does Nick's phys-'ical image blend easily with those in the family photo album, where his grandfather and great-grandfather, in dress uniform, strike poses of imperial splendor, their chests layered with war medals and crossed with ceremonial sashes.

Nick Arkas is a big, dark, shaggy-headed man with a friendly manner, brown eyes, and a stubble of beard. Although he is chief highway designer for the state and has an office in the capitol complex in Augusta, he dresses in the rough-and-ready style of an outdoorsman: checked shirt, jeans, boots, and a Dutch bargeman's cap set at a rakish angle. And he prefers to be outdoors, conferring with the road crews, when he has the opportunity.

Nick has never set foot in the Ukraine. Born in 1940 in a Ukrainian exile enclave near Prague, he moved with his parents to a similar neighborhood outside Paris eight years later, following the Communist takeover in Czechoslovakia. He was eighteen when his family immigrated to the United States. His accent and style of speech—blunt, funny, and earthy—are those of a street-wise New York, acquired during two decades of living and working in the boroughs of Greater New York.

Yet deep springs of Ukrainian nationalism flow strongly in Nick as in his forebears, one of whom gave up the epaulets of admiral in the Russian fleet rather than renounce the right to celebrate his Ukrainian language and culture. Nick's move to the small town of Gardiner, Maine in the mid-1970s in no way dimmed his nationalist ardor; in fact, Maine offered him a new and unexpected role: helping young Ukrainians escape from Russia.

Although the Arkas family has been prominent in Ukrainian cultural and nationalist circles for over a hundred years, the name itself is Greek, not Ukrainian. "My great-grandfather came to the Black Sea port of Nikolayev as a young Greek immigrant in the 1830s. He got into commerce right away, and began making money. He was also a linguist . . . published a commercial dictionary with translations into sixteen languages. So he got some contract work with the navy, doing translations."

Since Nikolayev was home base for Russia's Black Sea fleet and the site of a major naval academy, a growing family connection to the navy was both natural and profitable. "My great-grandfather graduated from the naval school and eventually became not only an admiral, but also an aide to Tsar Alexander II [1855–1881]. He also organized a commercial steamship company that got a monopoly on Russian trade with the whole Ottoman Empire. And he did a smart thing: he made the Tsar his business partner. So the Tsar got his cut. That's where the family's money came from. My great-grandfather is the one who built the family mansion." A photograph shows an elegant stone house of classical design facing a city square.

The admiral, despite his growing wealth and close association with the Tsar, was by no means an armchair officer. "He was an active commander, and took part in many battles. He even took my grandfather on his ship as cabin boy. One day in battle a cannon blew up and a piece of cannon ball lodged in his stomach. It stayed there all his life. My father remembered seeing this lump under my grandfather's skin."

In spite of that early trauma Nick's grandfather, too, followed a career in the navy and became an admiral in the Black Sea fleet. But he was both financially independent and deeply involved in other activities—particularly in promoting Ukrainian nationalism, which engaged him far more than promoting his own career.

"My grandfather knew that Ukrainian language and culture had been suppressed under the Tsars. Ukrainians had been made to feel they were an inferior people . . . they were called *malo Russ*—little Russians—in an empire that was dominated by Great Russians. The Ukrainian language was considered a peasant dialect, a crude offshoot of Russian. So Ukrainian literature and history had not developed much.

"He wanted to make Ukrainians proud of their own heritage. He collected a lot of stories from the past and wrote a popular history, *A History of Ukrainian Russians*. It was the first to be published in the Russian Empire, and the first to be written in Ukrainian. He had to bribe the Russian censors to allow its publication. It came out in 1907. After the Tsar's ethnic policies relaxed a little, the book was used in a program called *prosvita*, to bring education to the Ukraine's villages.

"After that he wrote an opera, called *Katerina*, in Ukrainian. He did it without any formal musical training whatever, which was amazing . . . just picked out notes on the piano . . . 'Oh, yeah, *that* sounds good.' It was based on a poem by Shevchenko, who is a sort of Ukrainian national bard. It was performed in the big opera house in Nikolayev. It was well-publicized, since it was the first opera ever written and sung in Ukrainian. There was standing-room only downstairs, which was filled with sailors and other common people; the rich and educated sat in the boxes.

"At that time my grandfather was already a full admiral. So he and the other Navy brass wore their dress uniforms, including their medals and dress-swords. During the intermission the Commander of the fleet called my grandfather over to his box. He told him it was 'inappropriate'—that's what he said, 'inappropriate'—for an admiral under his command to write an opera in Ukrainian. My grandfather got so mad . . . he shouted at the Commander, 'This is more important to me than my sword and rank. If you don't like what I've done, I'll resign from the Navy. Here's my sword.' Then he unbuckled his sword and scabbard and handed it to him.

"Well, my grandfather stayed on in the navy for awhile. But of course, he went down in rank after that episode. He couldn't have cared less. The navy had never been his main interest. There's a park in Nikolayev which has a plaque dedicated to my grandfather. Not for his career in the navy—that's not even mentioned—but for his contribution to Ukrainian literature and culture. *That's* what his real interest was."

A few years after the grandfather's death, his family experienced a dramatic testament to his impact on the common people of the Ukraine. "It was during the civil war, which was a confusing time for *everybody*. There was the Red Army and the White Army and a Ukrainian army and independent Cossack armies under local *atamans* . . . fighting going on all over the southern Ukraine. My grandmother knew it was too dangerous to go on living in the family mansion. So she and my father, who was a teenager, moved into an apartment with relatives.

"One day the ragtag army of a local *ataman*, a man named Bashkiriava, occupied the city. My father had already seen them come into town . . . on foot, poorly equipped, with sawed-off shotguns, et cetera. A couple of days later they started going house-to-house, collecting 'taxes' from people on the spot. So one day there was a knock on the door, and there stood a handful of these guys—peasants dressed in sheepskins—with a sailor in charge. He was very polite, spoke Ukrainian, asked, 'Do you have anything of value? Do you have anything to eat?' My grandmother said, 'We're happy to share what we have with you.' They sat down and ate sausages and bread. Then the sailor saw a picture of my grandfather. And he said, 'Are you related to *him*?' My grandmother said, 'Yes, that's my late husband.' 'Oh,' said the sailor, 'I'm sorry. Boys, there's nothing here for us to look for. These are *our* people.' And he tells my grandmother, 'Sorry for the inconvenience,' and they left without taking *anything*. And that is because of my grandfather's work with Ukrainian history and his opera . . . the sailor apparently had enough ethnic awareness to recognize him in the picture.

"My father, too, was born and raised in Nikolayev. Went to the naval academy, because that was the family tradition. But he didn't want a navy career. Anyway, he was drafted into General Denikin's

White Guards—a Great Russian force—when the civil war began. He refused an officer's commission . . . he didn't like serving in a Great Russian army anyway, and was just waiting for a chance to defect to a Ukrainian army where his brother served. But he never got the chance." In early 1920 Denikin's forces were defeated and its remnants evacuated to the Crimea where another White army, under General Wrangel, still held out. In the Crimean campaign, the Whites' futile last stand, Nick's father had his closest brush with death. "When he had left home he felt that he would never see it again. So he'd taken whatever he could carry in his knapsack . . . family pictures and documents, and the family crest. And in one very confused battle a Bolshevik sailor came up behind him and stabbed him in the back with a bayonet, which went right through his knapsack. The thrust knocked him down, and his attacker kept on going. But the bayonet struck the family crest, which was mounted inside a solid brass box. And that stopped the bayonet . . . it didn't even scratch him. But you can still see the dent it made in that thick brass plate.

"My grandfather on my mother's side also served in the Crimea, but as a civilian. He was a banker, and was appointed Finance Minister in an anti-Bolshevik government there which lasted less than a year. When a Red offensive forced them to evacuate the Crimea, the survivors, including my mother and her parents, went first to Turkey, and eventually settled in Czechoslovakia.

"My mother went to a Russian school in Prague. Her father wanted her to have a good education, so she went to Charles University and got a degree. There she met my father, who was getting his Ph.D. His dissertation was on Ukrainian history. They met at a Ukrainian Cossack reunion of some sort, and were married in 1938. I was born two years later.

"We lived in a large Ukrainian community—almost a whole Ukrainian government-in-exile—in this little village of Revnice, about twenty miles from Prague. There was every political shade, from White to Red, every political party represented. Teachers, professors from the University. Some people later died fighting *for* the Germans, others *against* the Germans.

"My father took odd jobs to earn a living, including tutoring and translating. He translated the *Iliad* and the *Tale of the Hosts of Igor*, an ancient Russian saga, into Ukrainian. And he wrote on Ukrainian history. He refused to write in any language but Ukrainian . . . probably could have made a good living for the family if he had been willing to write in Russian.

"When World War II came along a lot of Ukrainians saw the Germans as offering a chance to create an independent Ukraine. My father wouldn't support them, because of their treatment of the Jews. Our house had a cellar, like a little cave, under the regular basement. I remember people coming into the house at night and being hidden, whole families, in that little cave. A tunnel led into the woods, where someone would meet them and lead them out. Those people would offer my father diamonds, money . . . all sorts of things for his help. But he always refused. 'Just get in there,' he would say, 'and if you get caught later, just don't say where you came through.' Later my father joined the Czech underground as an aide to a man named Kruschka who headed the underground for our area.

"We stayed on after the war, but in 1948 the Communists took over the country. By then Soviet security officials had moved in, and were interviewing all émigrés, especially Russians. Our family was interviewed twice. They were mainly after socialists; monarchists and other fringe groups were left alone because they weren't considered much of a threat to the regime.

"But the N.K.V.D. were torturing other people. My uncle was a Social Democrat, and educated. He was taken to a Soviet concentration camp for almost a year. When he came back he was a different person . . . physically, morally, mentally broken. A little while after coming home he committed suicide.

"I guess my father's activities in the Czech underground during the war kept him from being sent to Siberia. He had been given a medal and was on the list of 'Heroes of the Czech Republic.' And he wasn't a socialist. So at first they let us alone. Little by little, however, the N.K.V.D. were pulling out the more educated Russians, regardless of their politics. So in 1948 the local Czech authorities, who were my father's friends, told him 'They,' meaning the Russians, 'are putting the screws on us. You *must* get out. Otherwise, they'll be sending you to the U.S.S.R.'

"So they arranged with the International Refugee Organization for us to immigrate to the West. We got a visa for France, and permission from the Czechs to leave within thirty days. In January 1949 we boarded a train for France.

"Two rail lines went west from Prague. One went through the Soviet-controlled zone of Austria, then Switzerland and France. The other went through Bavaria without going through the Soviet zone. We wanted to be sure to board the one going through Bavaria, because friends of ours who had taken the other route had vanished between Prague and the Swiss border.

"It was snowing, and we watched the stations go by. After a while my father said, 'Those stations aren't on the way to Bavaria; we're going toward Austria.' Late at night the train stopped. It was eerie . . . we were in the middle of a field, barbed wire on both sides, strobe lights making it like daytime, and men in fur coats and hats, with dogs and machine guns, walking back and forth, guard towers in the distance. Then Soviet officers came aboard to check passports. My father said, 'Well, this is the end.' He said good-bye to my mother and me, took clothing and shaving stuff out of the suitcase—what he figured he'd need in Siberia. Then we heard footsteps outside the compartment, and a knock at our door. And the biggest person I have ever seen came in—he looked like the abominable snowman—a big coat, big fur hat, a submachine gun slung over his shoulder. Very politely he asked for our passports and started to examine them. My mother and I were okay, because ours gave our nationality as 'Czech.' But my father's said 'Ukrainian,' because he was one of a few people who were citizens of the old Ukrainian Republic of 1918; so that could spell trouble. Then my mother noticed that the officer was looking at the passport upside down. He handed them back, saluted, said 'Thank you. Have a nice trip.' And left! We heard shouts down the corridor . . . they took some people off the train. Then it started up, went faster. My mother said, 'Maybe we've made it.' After a while it stopped again, and some customs officials came in wearing the little Swiss pillbox hats. And we all laughed and hugged each other. But my father aged ten years on that trip."

In France the family first stayed in a chateau outside Paris run by a Ukrainian relief organization. Each family had a room. Later they moved into a house nearby. Both parents found work, and Nick went to school.

The environment in which young Nick grew up there was, like their neighborhood in Prague, a hotbed of Ukrainian nationalism. "The house where we lived was owned by two old women: one was the widow of a man named Prokopovitch—the last Ukrainian prime minister, back in 1920; and the other was the widow of Simon Petlura, Ukraine's short-lived dictator in 1918. Old generals and politicians would visit, talking politics and plotting actions against the Soviet regime in the Ukraine. I even held in my hands the blood-stained shirt that Petlura was wearing when he was shot. I listened to all that talk by my father and his friends. As a kid, I didn't understand it all. But the idea of fighting for Ukrainian independence seemed romantic and adventurous to me. I've always looked at nationality as an extension of the family . . . honor, duty, and Ukrainian patriotism were of course very important to my father.

"Anyway, when I was sixteen I went to a French military school. By then I had become active in local Ukrainian organizations and I thought military training might be useful someday in helping to liberate the Ukraine. This was around 1956, when the Hungarians rose up against Soviet rule. The French government had quietly organized military training for young refugees from the U.S.S.R. and Eastern Europe. But by 1958 the French were putting some of those guys in the Foreign Legion—which was supposed to be all-volunteer—and sending them to fight the rebels in Algeria. I had no interest in that. So we thought it was time to leave France and come to the U.S."

They arrived in New York on the French ship *Liberté*. "People from the Ukrainian Red Cross were waiting to interpret for us and help us through Customs. An immigration official asked my father, 'Are you a Communist? Did you ever take up arms against the U.S.A.?' My father looked at him and said, 'Are you serious?' 'Yes.' 'The answer is *no*,' said my father. 'Well, welcome to the U.S.' Then my father said, 'Do you think I'd be crazy enough to say yes, even if I *had*?' He could not understand why they asked questions that no one would be foolish enough to answer the wrong way."

The family lived with Nick's aunt in New York City while they looked for work and an apartment. The language barrier ruled out any but menial jobs, and all three found work in a local hospital. "At first we always got the lowest-paying jobs. My father went from being a professor to being a janitor. But that *did* leave him time to write. He was offered a position teaching Russian at the U.S. Air Force Academy, but he felt he didn't speak English well enough. It was difficult financially. But we were glad we came. My parents always said we had to think how much worse we would have lived in the U.S.S.R. My father was completely happy with his books and his cats. My mother was the same. They were very private people . . . had few American friends.

"I went to high school . . . took enough courses, mostly English, to get a diploma. Then I went to work at Telesignal Corporation. We did wiring for the first U.S. space capsule. I stayed with them ten years. By 1970 I had twenty to twenty-five people working for me. When the Vietnam War ended, the work slowed down. So I quit and went to N.Y.U. at night and drafting school during the day."

He began work as a cartographic draftsman with Cities Service International, eventually becoming chief draftsman. He also translated French and Russian cartographic material for the company, and composed a cartographic dictionary in four languages. But he balked at being transferred to Tulsa. "I couldn't see it. So I quit, and took a job with the phone company in Buffalo. I commuted from Long Island. Every Sunday at 5:00 p.m. I'd take the train to New York, jump on a bus and ride to Buffalo. I'd check in at the local YMCA, then go to work. Friday at 4:00 p.m. I'd grab my suitcase, catch the bus, and go home."

Meanwhile Nick had married an Afro-American woman, a native New Yorker of Caribbean background. Two sons were born during the 1960s. "The commuting to Buffalo put too much of a strain on the family. So I quit. If my wife had been willing to move to Buffalo, I would have stayed on there."

In New York Nick and his father again became extremely active in Ukrainian affairs. "There was a Ukrainian Center at that time, near the Natural History Museum. I'd drive my father there to give talks in the evening. And we always had Ukrainian writers and poets and politicals coming to the house. Some were active in the

Ukrainian liberation movement, so I got involved with them, whether it was the flakiest or the most reasonable ones. They put me in touch with the Ukrainian youth movement in the U.S.S.R. It was an education for me. Whoever would come over, I'd get stuck working with them on some project of theirs. I wrote articles on the Ukraine for *Newsday*, and monitored the other papers, writing the editors when I read something I felt was untrue about the Ukraine.

"The liberation groups *here* were mainly concerned with raising public awareness about the political situation in the U.S.S.R. and particularly the differences between the various ethnic groups. And there were letter-writing campaigns, favoring United States support for the liberation movement.

"My father was more literary. In 1969 he published a 350-page *History of the Northern Black Sea Region*, covering the area's history from Paleolithic times to the third century B.C. And that was only volume one.

"In the early 1970s my parents moved to Maine. They rented a little house in Richmond, where some friends from New York had settled. I came up one summer with my kids, and I liked it here. So I told my wife, 'Look, I want to go to Maine. If everything works out, maybe you can come too.' Well, she didn't want to come . . . she'd spent all her life on Long Island . . . so we ended up getting a divorce. In 1976 I moved here permanently. My kids stayed with their mother, but spent their summers with me." Nick notes "the big cultural divide between my mother, who comes from a traditional Ukrainian background, and my son in his mid-twenties, who has grown up in a black culture in New York. They got along, but by staying out of each other's way. The gap in understanding was generational, too."

Nick seems reluctant to say much about his marriage. There was no parental pressure against it, he says, although his mother had earlier tried to arrange a match with a girl from a prominent Ukrainian family. "We liked each other, but any possibility of romance was killed when both sets of parents were pushing it. It would be fun to see her again, find out what her life has been like. I heard she was divorced, too.

"I didn't work for awhile after coming up here . . . just helped my parents run the house. And I did translations and maps for my father.

That kept me busy, because he got several books out. I didn't realize then how large a Ukrainian community there is here, because my father was doing his research and writing, and wasn't very involved with other people up here.

"In Richmond my parents had no American friends, except for one neighbor. They got along fantastically with them. My father didn't speak any English, but he spoke perfect Russian. They would meet once in awhile with Russian or Ukrainian friends. Otherwise, they were very self-sufficient. Some people have to have a big social life, have to go places, get dressed up. My parents were different. With them it was, 'Oh my God, guests. I'll have to put on a jacket.' Neither of them drove. My mother took the bus once a week to Gardiner to do the shopping. That was the big social event of the week, because all the Slavs were on the bus. She worked in her garden, walked the dog, looked after the cats, took care of my father's clothes. My father would go for long walks in the woods . . . his eyesight was so bad, he would sometimes get lost and my mother would have to go find him. Once he walked from Richmond to Gardiner along the tracks, about three miles, then came up on the road and was lost. Luckily the police dispatcher who found him was Belorussian and brought him back. He was eighty-three when he died.

"My first job here was with Clarostat, an electronics factory in Richmond. I applied for other jobs and after a few months I got one with the state, surveying roads. Later they transferred me to the head office, where I've been working for sixteen years. I'm the chief designer of roads for the state.

"I didn't know any local Ukrainians when I moved up here. I met the first ones through my father. He wasn't active himself as he grew old. But he was known through his writings and the family name. So they would come to visit him and argue politics. I'd get up to leave, but they would say, 'No, we want your son to stay.' They figured I would continue in my father's footsteps.

"One day I was talking with some Ukrainian friends and I said, 'We ought to have a Ukrainian organization here.' And they said, 'There already *is* one; it has a charter and everything.' It had been organized by a man named Krochmaluk—his son Andy still lives in Richmond—who had edited a newspaper in the Ukraine in the

1930s. He was a little rigid, a little dictatorial. Anyway the organization had gone dormant, so I hadn't known anything about it. So when Krochmaluk was visiting my father one time I said, 'Let's have a meeting and revive the organization.' He wasn't very enthusiastic. But we met and named it the Association of Ukrainian-Americans in New England. Krochmaluk was elected president. That was in 1978. We did not affiliate with any other Ukrainian organizations. We had around 150 members throughout New England and forty or so in the Richmond area. It included several doctors, lawyers. Most members were five to fifteen years older than me. Five or six of us, mostly younger guys, were really active. I was secretary for God knows how many years, because most of the older board members didn't write English that well."

Nick's father had reservations about an organization whose members, he knew, held strong and diverse political views. "He said, 'Okay, you tell *me* about the Ukraine; that's fine. But I already know a lot. So we're just going to get into an argument, because we have different ways of seeing things politically. Your association should go *outside*, and tell the American people about the Ukraine.' I felt the same way. So that's what we decided to do. We stayed away from issuing statements on Ukrainian politics. Our work has been mainly cultural and fundraising . . . we contributed money to a chair of Ukrainian studies at Harvard . . . we try to preserve the culture, the language.

"At first, when each of us went out to get other Ukrainians to join, they asked, 'Well, what are you guys going to do?' When we told them it would be cultural, educational activities, they said, 'Oh, yeah . . . that boring stuff.' Then we said, 'There will be picnics, too.' 'Ah, food and drink; music and dancing—that sounds good.' So we got real interest with that.

"One year we organized a supper and dance which we held in the hall of St. Nicholas, the other Orthodox Church in Richmond. Lots of Cossacks and Belorussians and Ukrainians and Great Russians were parishioners. We decorated it with bunting and the national flags of all those peoples. I asked one of the old Cossacks what the Don Cossack flag looked like. He told me it was yellow, blue, and white. He was really tickled when we displayed it at the party. 'You know, I've been living here all these years, and nobody has put up the Don Cossack flag before.' I said, 'Well, that's *your* fault. Don't wait for somebody else; *you* put it up.'

"Sometimes there was a little friction with the [local] Slavophile Society. We told the people who had organized it in the 1960s, 'You can't have the word "Slavophile" in the name and expect Ukrainians to participate. That word suggests Great Russian domination, support for the Russian Empire.' The original Slavophiles, in the 1850s, were Great Russian chauvinists. And the attitude of the local society was very much pro-Great Russian. When they talked about something it was always *Russian* culture, *Russian* writers. Three Ukrainians, including me, were on the board for awhile. But we all quit together. It was mainly the name, but also the policy. We tried to explain it to the others, but they didn't want to listen."

Members of the Ukrainian-American Association and the Slavophile Society continued to attend each other's picnics and parties, although ethnic and political frictions sometimes surfaced at such gatherings. At one party, Nick recalls, "Some of the Slavophiles said, 'You Ukrainians always start trouble. If it wasn't for you wanting to separate, Russia would be a great nation. Why do you guys think you're so much better than everybody else? You always want to pull out . . . out of the Slavophile Society, out of the Russian Empire . . . you always want to have your own thing.' I say, 'So, what's wrong with *that?*' 'Well,' they say, 'we could all join together and be a great nation.' And my answer is, 'Fine. You can all join Ukraine. We'll have one Great Ukraine. Why does it have to be a Great Russia, why not a Great Ukraine?' No, they don't want to hear that, you know. But I was just pulling their leg, because you have to be a realist.

"Another time we were having a joint celebration with them, a dance at the armory. One of the Slavophiles was attending bar. One of our guys goes to buy a drink and asks, 'Are you Russian?' The guy says no, he's a Serb. So our guy says, 'I'm Ukrainian.' And the bartender says, 'What's a Ukrainian? Ukrainians don't exist.' So our guy reaches over and bangs his face against the bar. He runs to complain to John Wlodkowski, the Slavophiles' president. John says to me, 'Hey, one of your guys is beating up one of ours.' But the guy hadn't told John that he'd insulted the Ukrainian first."

From Nick's account it is clear that these and similar incidents grew out of overheated ethnic pride and sensitivities, often heightened by alcohol. Petty as they seem, they nonetheless contributed to a growing distance between the two organizations.

The Slavophile Society had been extremely active at one time, even buying land with the idea of building a center near Dresden and homes for retired people there. Those plans never materialized, however, and the society gradually faded into obscurity. Although Nick attributes this in part to what he sees as the society's Great Russian bias, he also acknowledges the role played by personality clashes between its leaders and those of the Ukrainian-American Association. "Maybe with different people and more understanding on both sides," he concedes, "it would have worked, would have survived." Those remarks, together with the appearance of John Wlodkowski, former President of the now defunct Slavophile Society, at recent Ukrainian-American Association picnics, suggest that any personal animus between the two groups has long since faded.

Meanwhile Nick keeps abreast of political developments in the Ukraine. He speaks with authority about the 1994 national election and the leading parties and presidential candidates. He declines to identify which party he supports, but acknowledges there is one.

His political activism has found its major outlet, however, in assisting young Ukrainian defectors. "It started in July 1992, when I got a call from Father Kramarenko, an Orthodox priest in Portland, who said two Ukrainian sailors had just jumped ship from a Russian fish-processing vessel, the *Dauriya*. So I went down to the I.N.S. [the U.S. Immigration and Naturalization Service] office there to talk with them. The two young guys had apparently been treated pretty badly on the boat because of their nationality. The Captain and crew were mainly Great Russian. But their treatment was more a personal thing against Ukrainians than it was official policy. Anyway, the local I.N.S. people released them to the local Ukrainian community without requiring bail. And they allowed them to file for asylum in spite of the absence of formal 'political oppression.'

"Meanwhile we were arranging for all the legal work. We got a law student from Boston University to apply to the court for political asylum. I did most of the research and interpreting. Val Bardash [another member of the association] did a lot of the phoning, making contacts. Father Kramarenko called a press conference—we needed all the publicity we could get—and I interpreted. And it was continuous like that for the first six or seven weeks . . . newspaper interviews, TV appearances . . . I spent seventy or eighty hours on the case during that time. Later my friend Val Bardash took over that responsibility.

"We solicited money from Ukrainians outside Maine, so we could give the guys $100 a week expense money while we helped them find work. We got them a work permit, and in November '92—four months after they jumped ship—they started working full time in a warehouse in Augusta, and we got them into an adult ed class to learn English. They were self-sufficient from then on, and eventually they were granted political asylum."

In July 1993—a year after the first ship-jumping episode—the *Dauriya* again entered Maine waters and again lost two Ukrainian sailors through defection. This followed by a few weeks the defection of several other crew members, not all Ukrainians, when the ship docked in Canada.

"The *Dauriya* was spilling sailors like a farmer sowing seed," says Nick. "Our two guys had persuaded a Maine fisherman, who had delivered fish to the *Dauriya*, to take them ashore near Portland. This time the I.N.S. was hard-nosed. They said these guys might be criminals trying to escape prosecution—they had tattoos on their arms, like many Soviet criminals. Anyway, the I.N.S. required $3500 bail before releasing them to our priest." Three years later the two later defectors were working, but had not been granted asylum.

Nick mused about his work with Ukrainian asylum-seekers, then described his own political attitudes in contrast to those of his father. "I'm more radical, more hotheaded. My father was willing to wait. I'm not. My attitude is more like Arafat's: whatever is needed to gain attention, *do* it.

"It was funny . . . toward the end of his life my father and I didn't get along well. I mean, we respected each other; but we had completely different ideas of how to approach Ukrainian politics. He was always more academic, always the absent-minded professor. Give him books and stamps and he's happy. And he was more settled, maybe more disgusted with the whole subject, more pessimistic. I was more active, more optimistic, more violent. My father belonged to the Hetman party—a conservative party that favors a hereditary monarchy with some democratic aspects, and close economic ties to Moscow. But we—i.e., the Ukraine—don't need close ties to Russia. That would just mean Great Russian domination all over again. We have the grain, we have the industry. As far as I'm concerned, they could dig a big ditch between Ukraine and Russia and that would be okay with me."

During his work in behalf of the Ukrainian defectors Nick received several anonymous telephone threats. "One was a caller who spoke English with a really thick Ukrainian accent. He told me 'Don't even *think* about coming to the Ukraine.' There were others . . . crude crank calls late at night." These events, as well as the high cost of airfare, have inhibited Nick from visiting the Ukraine—a country he has never seen. Yet, beyond his lifelong fascination with the Ukraine, he has a strong personal mission to carry out there. "I want to bury my father's ashes there, in the family crypt in Nikolayev. If I don't get there maybe my son will do it some day."

CHAPTER EIGHT

A TALE OF TWO FARMERS' DAUGHTERS:
YELENA'S AND ANNA'S STORIES

YELENA SCHUMEJKO AND ANNA SIDELINGER have been friends since their primary school days in Richmond. They share similar backgrounds: both were born overseas in the early 1950s to Belorussian immigrants, both were of preschool age when they arrived in the United States, and both were raised on farms outside Richmond. They both began school with no knowledge of English.

Yet as each describes her experience growing up and her response to that experience, the two women might have been raised on different planets. Anna had a happy childhood and an easy transition to adulthood. She had no problems with her identity as a first generation Russian-American moving into the mainstream of American life.

Things were different for Yelena. She experienced a lonely, unsettled childhood and a troubled adolescence. Her "Russianness" was a source of confusion and denial until her mid-twenties, when she suddenly experienced an astonishing ethnic epiphany. She credits that event with bringing a sure sense of her identity and the start of a gradual turnaround in her life.

Yelena is a large, handsome woman. She speaks with animation, which is heightened by the musical timbre of her voice and by an occasional widening of her gray eyes to dramatize a point. A tinge of gray in her cascade of dark-brown hair is the only clue that she has left her thirties well behind.

Recently, for the second time in her life, Yelena has come back to live in Richmond after a prolonged absence—in this instance more than twenty years. "I've always loved this place," she says, nodding toward the small frame bungalow her father built thirty years ago. Set in a copse of tall pines and sugar maples, the house faces on a quiet country road seventy yards down the drive. Richmond village lies three miles to the east. "I would have come back here long before now if I'd known that my mother bought the house from my Dad years ago." Her mother, a victim of Alzheimer's disease, wandered aimlessly in and out of the house as we talked. She looked young for someone approaching ninety. Two affectionate young geese vied for Yelena's attention, waddling across our feet and tripping over the tape recorder. Their insistent peeping threatened to drown out our conversation.

Yelena's parents met in Munich at the end of World War II. "They were married in 1950, a short time after I was born. My father was sixty at the time, and my mother was forty-two. It was the second marriage for both. He had spent eight years in a Soviet prison camp in Siberia in the 1930s, and totally lost touch with his first wife and children. Somehow he managed to escape and find his way to Germany, where he worked as a carpenter.

"My mother was living in the Ukraine when the Germans invaded. They sent her to forced labor in a factory in Munich. Her early life had been hard . . . she had what was probably polio, and didn't walk until she was four. She was considered the 'slow' one of the eight kids. When she was eight, her mother died, and she was the one who stayed home to cook and clean house for her father. It was too much responsibility for a little kid. Then she married a handsome young accountant, but he turned out be an alcoholic and an embezzler. They had a son, but in the late 1930s she got a divorce and left them."

Yelena attributes her mother's later instability as a parent to those early experiences. "As I look back, she always seemed to have this streak of irresponsibility in her . . . there were times when she'd suddenly bolt the family—there were just the three of us—and take off on her own without saying a word. She could be gone for weeks. And she was distant in other ways, too. I felt her love was there, but a distant one, not a warm one."

Yelena and her parents came by freighter to the United States in 1951. "I still have the little trunk my father made as a crib for me to travel in. They moved around a lot the first couple of years . . . Colorado, New York, New Jersey. My early life, what I remember of it, began here in Richmond, where we came in 1953, when I was three years old. We were one of the first Russian families to settle here.

"My father had already managed to save $8,000, so he bought twenty-six acres with a big farmhouse. No central heating, no indoor plumbing. I think Poushental played a helping hand, because he was the only one around who spoke both Russian and English. My Dad moved us in, bought a cow and some chickens, handed my mother the keys and said, 'I'm going back to work.' She didn't know which end was which with a cow—*he's* the farmer, *she's* the city girl—then he went back to New York!"

A Russian woman living nearby helped Yelena's mother learn to take care of the cow and chickens that first summer, which Yelena remembers mainly for the swarms of black flies. Later that year her father quit his New York job to live at home full-time. "So my Dad started a *real* farm . . . he built a large chicken shed, got a few more cows, ducks. And the farm was what sustained us. We raised vegetables, made our own butter and cheese. I learned how to grade eggs and get them ready for the egg-man to pick up. And I milked the cows and once delivered a calf. My Dad also did carpentry for a local builder, Bernard Smith.

"Then I started school, the first grade. But I had just turned five . . . a little too young. I was the only Russian in my class, and because of the language I just wasn't catching on. So I was put back a couple of times in first and second grades. I had one American friend, Mary Lynch, who lived on the farm next to us. The Lynches were good friends . . . taught me American ways—hot dogs, baked beans. They moved to England when I was six or seven. Our farm was really rural then, just one other nearby; so I had no other children to play with."

Yelena recalls an almost complete absence of social contacts between her family and local "Americans"—i.e., non-Russians. "There was no organized socializing between the Russians and Americans, no community get-togethers or church suppers or anything like that. We were friendly with our neighbors. But I can't remember ever having an American person in our home sitting around talking with my parents. The only ones to come around were truck drivers delivering grain and things. The only American home I recall going into was the neighbors.'

"But we had lots of Russian friends come. Poushental would drop by . . . a loud, gruff man with a big laugh . . . and drink with my Dad, who made his own vodka. In the summer we rented rooms to Russians who came to spend their holiday in Richmond. My father had modernized the house. It had two bedrooms up and two down, a double kitchen, modern plumbing. When Russian families came with their children it was nice for me. Otherwise I was a little adult, because I was always with adults."

In their early years in Richmond Yelena's family, especially she and her mother, took part in some of the Russian-speaking community's activities. "My parents belonged to St. Alexander Nevsky Church, but not to other groups. We went to services regularly. Father Afanazi held religious classes, where I was the youngest. The Church had social events, like the *Yolka* at Christmas time. Everyone would get together and make *pirozhki* and other Russian dishes, and the children would recite poems or perform dances or songs. I always had to learn a poem for the *Yolka*—some are still rattling around in my head somewhere.

"And I have fond memories of the Belenkovs. He was an artist and she was a ballerina, a great woman. They and the Sherbakoffs were so talented . . . they put on skits that were unreal. I went to every play they put on, always in Russian. My mother and I played in some of their skits until my father forbade it. He thought some of the songs my mother sang were 'Communist' because they weren't the old ones *he* remembered . . . he was a generation older, of course, so he would mutter, 'You're singing a Communist song,' and walk out. He was so anti-Communist. I wasn't allowed to wear anything red until I was old enough to say, 'Hey, give it a rest.' But he had nothing to do with the White Russians, like the old *Corpus* members, here. And he had no love for the Russian aristocrats. They hadn't been through what he'd gone through."

Even as a preadolescent Yelena was expected to spend much time working on the farm—an activity that sometimes aroused fierce childish resentment. "It was a lot of work, and I was involved in *every-thing*, including shoveling cow-shit. There was this beautiful little blonde American girl, Patty, who came to all the Russian plays, with the most gorgeous patent-leather shoes. And I remember thinking as I was shoveling, 'I bet *Patty* doesn't have to shovel cow-shit.' But I'm glad now I did those things. It made me a better person to experience all that."

Soon, however, the Schumejko farm ran into serious financial problems, showing up on Richmond's list of tax delinquents for the first time in 1958. "My parents had little knowledge of English or financial dealings," Yelena says. "They trusted a lot of people, and at one point the grain supplier presented my father with an astronomical bill—$8,000—which he could not pay. I don't know just what happened financially. There was fraud somewhere along the line. But my father couldn't prove it, and I was too young to understand. Anyway, he went bankrupt.

"We hadn't been making it financially for some time. We were strapped. Had milk, butter, cheese, eggs, our own apples, so we weren't poor in *that* way. But we had no money to buy things."

Yelena has especially vivid memories of Christmas the year she was eight. "Well, we put up a Christmas tree. But we had *nothing* to put under it. *Nothing*. I remember finding an old beat-up wallet in the attic and wrapping it as a present for my Dad, and putting it under the tree. And my Mom wanted money to buy me some presents, but my Dad had only three dollars in his pocket. As a child, I just didn't understand it. So at one point a few days before Christmas, my Mom said to my father, 'You have *got* to tell her *now*.' So he pointed to this loft where he had his workshop, and said, 'Go up in the loft. There's something for you there.' And up there were shopping bags full of presents just for *me* . . . dolls and a doll-crib, toys . . . it was like Heaven. And I put them all under the tree. Well, it turned out that our delivery men, all Americans, saw that times were tough for us, and had pooled their money to buy toys for me. . . . I knew those men, and had been chitty-chatty with them. Since then I've wanted to thank them, but I didn't know their names. They probably never knew what a difference they had made for one little Russian kid's Christmas."

The bankruptcy brought immediate disruption to the family's relatively placid life. "My mother moved to South Boston to take a job at an electronics assembly plant. After my father locked up the farm we followed her there, and he went to work in a furniture factory. He was around seventy at the time. They did *not* lose the farm, however. They went to court, and he was paying around $25 a month to pay off the debt to the grain company.

"I lost a year's schooling with all the turmoil, and was put back a year. I was a latchkey kid before that title was popularized. I was on my own until 5:00 or 6:00 p.m. every day. We stayed there about three years—just long enough to accumulate the money needed to pay off the debt. Then we came back here to live on the farm again."

But all three, particularly Yelena and her father, had changed a great deal during the years in South Boston; their lives on the farm could not be the same as before. Her mother now commuted to work in a fish cannery in Bath, and her father had grown cranky and too old to farm. "We didn't really farm again. My father had a cow and a pig, and a garden. I helped him, but didn't want to do it any longer. And he was starting to get really ugly, angry at life in general. Maybe he was ill and we didn't realize it. He was unhappy with the priest, so he no longer went to church. He and my mother really didn't get along at all. Things got so bad my father moved into the upstairs apartment in the house and lived separately from us.

"By then my adolescence was hitting, and my father had become so unreasonable at that time about everything . . . he would have locked me up if he could. He refused to let me spend the night at the home of a girlfriend, but I went anyway. He made me wear opaque lisle stockings, not nylons. And no make-up. So I'd put the nylons and make-up in my purse and put them on at school, then remove them before going home. I remember going to a school dance with liquid aquamarine eyeliner in the shape of wings! It was done tastefully, so the school authorities didn't say anything. The other kids didn't wear much make-up. That was something that was just *me*. My mother allowed me to do these things. I always told her where I was going and what I was doing. But I did what I wanted. How can you listen to parents who are living in a different time zone . . . on a different planet? So yes, I rebelled."

Yelena's conflict over her ethnic identity also broke into the open at this time, causing further tensions with her father. "I'd only been away a couple of years, so the kids at school remembered me when I came back. I fit in again; but at the same time I *didn't* fit in. And I really wanted to. I'd always been aware that as a 'Russian' I was different. By the time I was eleven or twelve, that really got to me. I refused to *be* different, refused to knuckle under to it. I had to push myself in, I think . . . played basketball, was a cheerleader, took part in a dance group. So I wasn't an outcast. Adolescence is a tough time anyway.

"I hadn't picked up with the Church or former Russian friends or Russian activities after coming back to Richmond. I was living an *American* life by then, and didn't want any part of the Russian community here. But my Dad wanted me to be *Russian*, and that was all there was to it. So there were lots of blowups. One big one was over my hair, which was the longest hair in history and I *hated* it. One day I went to Tilly's Beauty Salon and had it cut off, really *chopped* . . . it was a perm that looked like a little Afro. I came home and walked into the kitchen, where my Dad was drinking a cup of coffee. He looked at me, and I could see his eyes get this raging look. He shouted, '*Gdyeh volosy? Chto vwee zdelali?*' (Where's your hair? What have you *done?*) I stayed calm. I said '*Svoyee volosy. Eto vsyo.*' (It's *my* hair. That's all.) My mother defended me, saying 'Oh well, she just wanted a new style hairdo.' I had told her I was going to do it. My father just wanted to control me, control my mother. But she rebelled, just as I did."

About this time, when Yelena was fourteen or fifteen, the family began to split up. "My father filed for divorce. My mother and I continued to live in the big farmhouse for awhile, and my father moved to *this* house, the smaller one he'd built. I think he got along better with her after the divorce. He no longer paid much attention to me, just let me go on my own. I'd go visit him on Sundays. There were still scenes . . . he'd hide in the bushes by our house, waiting for a young man to bring me home from square dancing, which he didn't approve of. He'd shout obscenities at me as I walked into the house.

"Then my mother left home, and began living with a man in Leominster, Massachusetts. I lived by myself in the farmhouse. Later, when my father found out, he made me move in with him, where I stayed six months. He closed up the farmhouse."

In 1966, at age sixteen, Yelena became pregnant. "It was a local boy. I was petrified over what my father might do if he found out. As soon as I knew I was pregnant, I left for Massachusetts. My mother had broken up with this other man by then, and was living in a large apartment with an elderly Russian lady. So I stayed with them until I could find a place of my own. I enrolled in the local high school and kept going until the last month. As a school child I had some social security money to sustain me. My mother moved into my flat. She was astonished when I finally told her I was about to have a baby. But she took it well. Russian people seem able to face reality.

"After Elise was born I went back and got my GED. Then I worked while my mother looked after the baby. When my mother got a job, I worked the night shift at a coffee and donut shop and stayed home with Elise during the day. So I spent three years—1967 into 1969—raising my child, with a lot of help from my mother. My father had moved to Florida by then."

In 1969, when Yelena was nineteen, she married an Italian-American man in his late thirties to whom she stayed married for nearly twenty years. "The first ten years of our life together were good. We had three children. He was a good father to them, and to Elise and his two from a previous marriage who didn't live with us. He made a good living. We had a house in the city and a summer place on the shore.

"But the last ten were a disaster. He was a cruel man, cruel emotionally. And he never wanted me to work . . . thought I should stay home, you know the saying, 'barefoot and pregnant.' And I had to account for every *penny* I spent. I'd been raised to believe females should be subordinate to males and submissive; but I no longer *felt* that way. So we had terrible arguments, and there was abuse. It was like being in your father's house and fighting your father, only now it was my husband."

The single big event in those years that Yelena recalls most vividly and in great detail is a trip to Boston Harbor in the summer of 1973 to see visiting ships from the Soviet Navy. She credits that serendipitous event with changing her feelings about herself and her life.

"My husband, who is very proud of his own ethnicity, urged me to go visit these Russian ships. They were docked right at the pier. So I took my mother, my sister-in-law, her daughter, and my three kids. There were long, long lines waiting to get on board. So I went up to this state trooper and said, 'Look, I'm Russian, my mother here is Russian, and we'd like to get on one of those ships. Do you really think, with all these kids, we have to stand out here in these long lines?' So he waves us through. I had to do the same routine at three different barricades. But finally we get to the exit ramp from one of the ships. Military personnel are standing there, and they look Russian. So I tap one on the shoulder and start speaking Russian to him. 'Oh, da!' he says, so I explain the whole thing again. He says 'Okay,' takes two of the kids by the hand, and off we go!

"We met all these Russian sailors, including one from my mother's hometown. It was so extraordinary. Then they brought some visiting U.S. sailors over, and asked me to translate. The Americans wanted the Russian guys to come over to their ship for dinner, et cetera. The Russians wanted to know all about me, what I did, and they were hugging my kids . . . it was just wonderful. And I met the Captain, talked with him awhile. By then it was late, so we left.

"When we got home I said, 'Mom, I'm going back tomorrow and go on that second ship.' So I got up early and went by myself. Got on the other ship the same way, only this time I was followed by two plainclothes guys, K.G.B. I'm sure.

"And I started talking with this young Russian sailor. There was immediate camaraderie . . . something just clicked. We asked each other questions. And I suddenly found there were *things I needed to know*. My parents would never talk to me about Russia . . . it was as if they had something to hide, something they were afraid to tell me because it might hurt me. So anyway, I asked this sailor what it was like to *be* there, in the U.S.S.R.; how did he *feel* about life, was he married, did he have children, did they believe in God. I wanted to know *everything* I could. I asked him what he'd do when his three-year navy was over. He said, 'There are two classes of people in our country: the educated and the plain worker. All I'm going to be is a plain worker. If you're lucky enough to get an education, you go on.' He was so honest about things, it was scary. By now others had gathered around, asking all sorts of questions. American sailors were coming aboard, and *they* started asking me, 'what does this mean, what does that mean.' And the Russians brought their band up, the sailors started singing. I knew some of the songs, and sang with them— 'Katushka', 'A Moscow Evening' . . .

"Then suddenly the Captain appears. Everybody stops. Cold turkey. It was like my private audience. I say 'Hello.' He says 'Good day'—very formal. All this in Russian. He's *very* serious. Up until then everyone has been smiling, but now they're all serious. And he asks me, 'Who are you?' I say, 'Who am I? Yelena Schumejko.' 'How do you speak Russian so well?' 'I'm Russian.' He gives me this look, and says 'From where?' So I give him the whole spiel on my background. 'Uh-huh,' he says. Then more questions. Are you married? Da. Children? Da. Where do you work? I don't work, I stay home and look after the children. Then he says, 'In Russia, all women work.' I say, 'But you're not in Russia now.' He didn't like that. And of course the whole crew is listening to all this. So finally he says 'Good day,' and goes off to another part of the ship.

"I stayed aboard another hour or more. Every other visitor was escorted quickly on and off. But I'm still there! And it was *the best day* . . . 'I'm Russian . . . *I AM RUSSIAN!*' It was like something had happened to me. I can't explain it. I wanted to stay on that ship and go with them. There is a piece of me that needs to connect there. It was wonderful. After that it was like, 'Here I am, world!'

"It was around when 6:00 or 7:00 p.m. when I left for home. I was emotionally raw, but exhilarated. I told my husband about it, and he said, 'C'mon, let's take the kids and go back.' Visits were over for the day, but a few people were on the pier, leaning over the rail and talking with crew members on the deck a few feet below. Three pretty girls were trying to communicate with them, so they got me to interpret. Soon the bow was filled with Russian sailors. Candy and cigarettes were passed down. It was getting dark by then, so I told the kids we had to go home. The sailors stood at attention and actually saluted me! And one of them took off his cap and gave it to me. Some Russian press photographers were there, taking pictures of the kids, and interviewing me. So I wished them all *'Schastlivaya doroga'*—a happy road ahead—and we left.

"And that's my memory. I cried for the next two weeks after that day. I'd lost something, and I'd gained something. I wanted to go with them, to find an identity. It was such a dramatic experience, it changed something in me. For awhile after that I couldn't relate to anybody . . . not *anybody* . . . I wanted to share the experience, but there was no one who would understand.

"From that day on I was never ashamed to be Russian. And I felt touched by all the Russian people I knew . . . my mother, my father, the sailors. There's always a reason for things to happen. It's brought something more to my life. I've had to put it on a back burner for awhile, because I had to raise my children and now I have to take care of my mother. But I have this feeling there's something I still have to do. I don't know yet what that is, except that it has to do with the Russian people. I think of all the suffering, the hardships they've been through. When I hear something about Russia now, it's like my own personal thing."

A few years after the Russian ship visit, Yelena took her first step toward a more independent life by accepting a job offer as assistant manager of a clothing store. "Opportunity knocked, so I took it. By then the kids were all in school. Later I was offered a better job with an expensive clothing store, and stayed with them quite a while.

"Meanwhile my personal life was in the pits. The problems with the marriage got worse . . . verbal abuse, physical abuse, and some things I don't want to go into. I stayed with him another ten years after all that began. Finally in 1988, when I was thirty-eight, I decided to leave my husband. By then the kids were either living away or were teenagers who weren't home much of the time anyway. I knew I was in a very destructive situation and had to get away.

"My mother was living here in Richmond by herself. So in April 1988 I came back up here for two weeks to be by myself and work things out. My mother had sold the big farmhouse and bought this smaller one from my father with the idea of leaving it to me one day. She hadn't told me. If I'd known about that when I had my first child, I'd have moved back up here with her then. I always had it in mind to come back here *some* day.

"It took me another year to finally leave. Subconsciously I was starting to move . . . bringing belongings up here each time I came to see my mother . . . a hutch, an old wood-stove . . . I realize now I was making my nest. But I needed a final push to make the break. I think that *push* was meeting Mike"—a Richmond man to whom she became engaged in 1992. "We met in August 1988. We weren't friendly at first. But later we did hit it off. He's such an honest person. He wasn't the *reason* for my leaving, but he was another thing drawing me back. So I filed divorce papers, and came up here for good in June 1989.

"I didn't do much for a year or two except take care of my mother, who was glad to have me back, and make the house livable for us. She was showing the signs of Alzheimer's disease by then. I cried a lot. The house was a disaster. It had been closed for ten years, so the toilet didn't work, the place was overgrown with weeds. My son Anthony was with me for the first few months, but chose to live with his Dad and where his friends are. I respected that, but it killed me . . . my youngest was graduating from high school, so I didn't expect her to move here. But I thought Anthony would be with me."

Gradually Yelena became more active in the community, although her mother's deteriorating mental condition ruled out any long-term commitments. "I took a job as bartender in the town's only restaurant, the Railway Cafe. It was fun, but after a year I found I had to spend more time with my mother. For a couple of years I organized the crafts fair for the town's annual Richmond Days celebration. And I started going to church again for awhile."

As one of St. Alexander Nevsky's few younger members who is fluent in both Russian and English, Yelena is occasionally called on as interpreter for the ever-more frequent groups of Russian visitors to the church. "Finally, after all these years, it's popular to be Russian. But I've *always* been Russian. It's important not to deny our heritage, to remember where we came from."Caring for her mother the past few years, however, left Yelena little free time, even for work in her home studio as an accomplished stained-glass artist. Nor did she feel free to marry Mike while her mother needed virtually her full-time attention. Like most local Russians, she preferred to keep her mother at home as long as possible. Meanwhile, Yelena and her fiancé built a new house on the property—an airy, redwood chalet with wide decks and picture windows overlooking fields and woods.

"I don't think I've *ever* been as content as I've been these past few years since coming back here." As she speaks two young geese nestle against her feet, peeping quietly. Odie, Mike's miniature Doberman, leaps into her lap and falls asleep.

In August 1996 Yelena's mother died. Following a full Russian Orthodox funeral, Mathilda Schumejko was buried under an oak tree within view of the new house. Mike made a traditional Orthodox wooden cross to mark the grave. Yelena married Mike in 1997.

✳ ✳ ✳ ✳ ✳

Anna Sidelinger is the Argentinian-born daughter of Basilio and Natalya Lepushenko, who came to the United States and settled on a chicken farm outside Richmond in 1959. Anna was then four years old. She was raised in a rural enclave of other Russian-speaking settlers that included her parents, siblings, both sets of grandparents, three married aunts and a married uncle, thirteen cousins, and several nearby Great Russian and Ukrainian families.

Anna's story is one of an immigrant child's successful and easy assimilation into the American mainstream. She earned a college degree, married a local Maine man, and in her mid-thirties was appointed manager of a local bank. After two hours of conversation with Anna, however, it was clear that she has also managed to retain strong ties to her ethnic and religious roots and is totally comfortable in her identity as a Belorussian-American.

Anna is friendly and brisk as she meets me in the foyer and leads the way to her office in Gardiner Savings. The bank fronts on Richmond's main street, two miles from her home. "Sorry I couldn't meet you for lunch, but we're in the middle of changing our computer system. I'm putting in sixty-hour weeks, helping out at some of the other branches. So I've been skipping lunch or snacking at my desk." Her dress, bronze-colored with a satin sheen, is conservatively feminine and ankle-length. Her light brown hair falls to her shoulders in soft curls. Her eyes are lively and engaging, her manner relaxed and down-to-earth. She speaks with animation of her childhood days as a tomboy, but disclaims any athletic prowess. "God, no; I'm too clumsy," she laughs. "We lived on Langden Road, about three miles outside town. It was a dirt road then, with no traffic. My grandparents, as well as my aunts and uncles and their families, had the farms stretching along both sides of ours. The Vaulins, the Supruniuks, and other Russian-speaking families also lived along the road. Even as little kids we could play in the fields, swim in Vaulins' pond, or fish in the creek, and still be within sight of a home where the people knew us. There were bikes and a horse to ride, and big yards where we played baseball. I had a dozen cousins to play with, plus friends we would bring home from school. There were always enough of our own age around, and older kids to keep an eye on the little ones.

"And there were big family celebrations, particularly in summer . . . a barbecue on the beach for someone's birthday, or when friends of my parents would visit from New Jersey. Often sixty people would be in our back yard, singing Russian folk songs, dancing, eating and drinking. On New Year's Eve they sometimes rented the Grange Hall for a potluck party, with records of Russian songs. My brother played the *baiyan*—a distinctive Russian accordion—and the *balalaika*. Both my mother and grandfather were good singers . . . both sang in the choir at church. We kids were allowed to invite special friends to the party, so there would be as many as thirty kids there. While the grown-ups sang and ate and talked and drank downstairs, we played games and found secret hiding-places in the Hall's upstairs. For us it was a rare chance to stay up as late as the adults.

"But we no longer do things like that. We haven't had a family reunion since my grandmother died eight years ago . . . the last of my grandparents to go. She was very special to me as I was growing up. She was like everyone's grandmother *should* be. I remember her always wearing an apron, and a kerchief around her head—a real 'babushka.' She would bake bread in an outdoor oven in the summer, and tell stories while I would swing from a big maple tree in her yard. She told me stories of life in old Russia, and Grandfather's experiences in the cavalry during the civil war there. But most of her stories were typical Russian fables, stories with a moral . . . 'be good and candy will fall from the sky.' And many were based in the Orthodox faith.

"My grandmother encouraged me to be independent and stand up for myself. Yet she was also the one who would report me to my parents when she saw me and other kids misbehave. Once, when I was eleven, she caught us under the house trying to smoke old cigarette butts. I hoped that she would live long enough to see my daughter. But she died three months before Riana was born.

"Every once in a while I like to drive back to Langden Road just to see the old farms and houses. It has changed so much. The road is paved. And none of my family live there now. One aunt still lives in Richmond but, except for my parents, all the others have moved away or died. So it always makes me sad when I go back to where we had such good times as children."

Anna went to Richmond's public schools, where her best friend was a non-Russian. "I never experienced any discrimination because of being 'Russian.' In high school I was a cheerleader and a member of the glee club. And I was active in the school theater group. One year we put on a murder mystery which we wrote ourselves. We called it 'Ruka'—Russian for 'hand.' It won first prize in a school drama contest in Boothbay."

She has continued to play an active role in the St. Alexander Nevsky Church since childhood. "We spoke Russian at home, particularly with my grandparents. But our church sponsored Russian language and culture courses for the children. We met in the church twice a month during the school year and twice a week in summer. Mr. Vaulin, who had taught college courses in Russian language and literature, taught us the alphabet. We had alphabet books and Russian storybooks. And the priest gave us Bible lessons. I can still read and write Russian, but not as well as I speak it. My mother and I are both active members of the church. We belong to its 'sisterhood,' which is like the altar guild in a Protestant church. We help keep the church artifacts clean, we bake for special holidays, and for the bake sale at the town's Richmond Days celebration each summer, things like that. And my mother still sings in the church choir."

After graduating from high school Anna enrolled in the University of Southern Maine, earning a degree in social work. Since then she has taken special courses in business and economics. "It was always assumed in our family that I would go to college, and that all of us— my brother and sister and I—would go on to professional careers. The only problem was how to finance the tuition costs. But we managed." Her sister Irene, now married to an electrical engineer and living in Massachusetts, was at one time employed as secretary to the director of Maine Medical Center. Walter, the youngest sibling, is working toward a graduate degree in electrical engineering at the University of Maine. Anna's husband is a third-generation Richmond man. "Richard and I were married in my church. I wouldn't have had it any other way. The service was conducted half in Russian, half in English out of consideration for Richard and his family. It was just assumed that we would raise our kids in the Orthodox faith. My husband, who sometimes went to Catholic services as a youth, was baptized in our church. Later he worked out an arrangement with my mother: she would teach him to speak Russian, and he would teach her to drive. He's picked up quite a lot of Russian, but she was pretty hopeless as a driver, so she gave up that idea."

Anna credits her parents with instilling in their children a pride and satisfaction in being who they are. It is clear that she still feels extremely close to both parents. "Politics is the only issue where my father and I really differ," she says. "I guess that's the one area where I showed my rebellion and independence. He's always been so conservative. And I can still make him angry over politics. Not long ago I cracked a joke about one of our recent U.S. Presidents, and my Dad got really mad, as I knew he would, saying that I was being disrespectful. But lately, with a growing daughter, I find that I'm getting more conservative myself!"

Anna, Richard, and their daughter, Riana, live on a property adjacent to her parents' home in a house built by her father. Richard is a crew chief with Maine's Department of Transportation. "During the day, while Richard and I are at work, my mother looks after Riana, who turned seven in 1996. Takes her in after school, and has taught her to speak Russian. And yes, she tells her the same Russian fables and stories that my grandmother told me. I would not want to live far from Richmond. This place has been too important in my life."

CHAPTER NINE

THE RELUCTANT ACTIVIST:
MICHAIL'S STORY

IN 1974 MICHAIL GRIZKEWITSCH, son of a former Soviet Army officer, moved to Richmond with his wife and two young daughters. For Michail, then thirty-two, and his American-born wife Virginia, it was a risky move. They were leaving the comfort of a modern suburban apartment and the security of well-paid jobs in Brockton, Massachusetts for a rundown farmhouse and uncertain job prospects in rural Maine.

They had compelling reasons to move, however. "I'd been working fifty-five to seventy hours a week in a machine shop for seven years," Michail recalls. "The pay was good. My salary there, twenty years ago, was what Bath Iron Works pays me now, in 1994. It was high-precision work, and there was good health insurance, food. There was even a bar in the shop. But most of my friends there were either alcoholic or suffering from various nervous conditions. So I could see what would happen to me if I stayed there."

He and Virginia had visited Michail's married sister in Richmond and liked what they saw, particularly the small-town, rural environment. "My boss even offered to buy us a house if I'd stay in Massachusetts. But we wanted to live here, and we wanted more land. So we bought our present house and fifty acres for $15,000. It needed a lot of work. The roof, supporting beams, and walls needed reinforcement or replacement. The barns were also in poor condition, and the land in back was a jungle." Michail, now in his early fifties, is a muscular man with thinning black hair, a mischievous smile, and an air of barely suppressed energy. It is 9:00 a.m., and he has just returned from the night shift at Bath Iron Works, where he is an ordnance machinist. He is wide awake, and more interested in conversation than in sleep.

"So coming here was a dumb move for us to make, yes?" But it is clear Michail doesn't believe that. Indeed, for him the move was only the latest in several uprooting changes in his life. Even his birth was in transit: it took place in 1942, in a farmhouse "somewhere in Belorussia," while his parents and young sister paused in their westward flight away from the warfare engulfing their homeland. The family was later taken to Germany and placed in a labor camp, where Michail spent the first three years of his life. "It was my mother's skills that saved us there. She had trained as a nurse."

With the end of the war they were uprooted again and found their way to a Displaced Persons camp near Hamburg. "My father applied for immigration papers for the United States. But as a couple of years passed and they hadn't come through, he grew afraid that we'd be forced to go to the U.S.S.R. instead." So when Michail was six or seven the family boarded a ship bound for an unknown destination in South America.

"We ended up in Brazil. That was lucky: Brazil needed skilled people, and my father was a carpenter and mason, and my mother was a seamstress. We were sent to Sao Paulo. In spite of the language barrier, both my parents found work right away. And we got no help from the government." In 1954, after living close to ten years in Brazil, Michail's parents took the opportunity to emigrate to the United States, where some old friends from home had recently settled. "I didn't want to go. By then I had friends, a trade, my school. And we were living well. Wages were very low, but food and housing were cheap. The United States had always been my parents' long-term goal, however, and finally there was a family there to sponsor us. So my father borrowed $2,000 from his American friends for the plane fare, and we left."

—126—

They settled in South River, New Jersey, where Michail found himself living in a Russian-speaking neighborhood for the first time in his memory. "In Brazil we'd lived by ourselves in a small town outside Sao Paulo where we were the only Russian-speaking family for miles around. The nearest Russian church was fifty miles away. But in South River, half the town was Russian. You didn't have to speak English to get along there. My father worked as a carpenter, but never learned English. Never *had* to. That made it especially easy for my parents. And we didn't need a car. Everything was right there, with people to help us if we needed it. The doctor spoke Russian, the dentist spoke Russian, they spoke Russian in all the stores."

A few years later Michail's parents separated. "My father was a heavy weekend drinker, and abused my mother. So my mother, my two sisters and I moved to an apartment on the outskirts of town, away from the Russian neighborhood." By then Michail had already established himself as an independent youth with no need or desire to bond with an ethnic community. In Brazil he had gone to a technical training school at an early age, and was working as a machinist at age fourteen. In the United States, however, he faced job restrictions and school requirements which he found frustrating, and which contributed to a sense of standing alone and a need to be self-reliant. "It seemed strange to me that no one would hire a boy of fifteen who was a qualified machinist with more than three years' technical schooling. So that first summer in the United States I did nothing but go fishing. To earn money I collected bottles and turned them in. I wondered why people here would throw away something they could get money for. Anyway, I earned enough to pay for movies and ice cream. I never ran out of money, and I didn't even have a job! That was one of the best summers of my life."

When Michail started school that fall, he was first put in the eighth grade. He still remembers that first day. "The English teacher gave a test, because she didn't think my English was good enough to be in that class. Well, I got a '50' . . . jeez, that was pretty good, you know? I'd beat the system! By then I knew a verb from a noun, mainly from the movies and TV. But it didn't work. They put me in the sixth grade for *all* my classes, because the teacher spoke Polish, and they thought I'd be more comfortable. But I wasn't comfortable *at all* . . . all the kids were so much younger. Anyway, after a few months they moved me to the seventh grade, and then back up to the eighth—so here I am, back in the same classroom with that same teacher. And she makes me take both seventh and eighth grade English in the same year."

After that first year his school day was split. "The lower school for English and history, then I walked a mile across town to the high school for science and math. I was the only kid in school with no free period. Mine was spent walking. But I was a good student."

Michail enjoyed sports, but was appalled by his introduction to American football. "The high school coach invited me to come out. So I show up. At that first practice, I couldn't believe it. The coach was actually teaching you to *annihilate* the other guy. I'd played soccer in Brazil, and you just don't *do* that in soccer . . . it only invites retaliation. And here the coach was saying 'Nail him!' I said no, I didn't think I wanted to get my body punished like *that.* So he asked me to kick the ball. I had no problem with that; I can kick a ball. But I said, 'After I kick the ball, what do I do?' And he said, 'Well, you duck because the other guys will nail you.' I ask, 'Who's going to be blocking for me?' 'Nobody.' But I'm not a nut. I refused."

Michail found a more congenial sports opportunity in nearby Brunswick, where a Hungarian soccer club invited him to play with them. "They were somewhat older guys. I played with them for two years. That led to some social life. Soccer players get written up in the local papers, too. By that time I was also playing basketball, for South River High."

Michail was too busy, and a little too old, to spend much time socializing with his high school friends, however. "I wanted to work. So I found a part-time job with the town's recreation department, and when I needed money for a special date or something, I went crabbing and sold my catch to local stores. Later I worked part-time as a carpenter, and learned to repair slate roofs. So I had very little time to hang around after school. I had my jobs, and I was dating Virginia by then. I didn't mix with the guys much."

Following graduation Michail, together with his mother and two sisters, moved to Massachusetts, where he found full-time work and took night courses at a technical school. In 1963, when he was twenty-one, Michail married Virginia, who came from a non-Russian background. By the time they moved to Maine nine years later, they both were confident they had skills that would be readily marketable in the Pine Tree state. As a precision machinist Michail has since then worked for the Neuroscience Corporation, and later for Aeromarine Company. He has produced the fine needles used in brain surgery, and microscopic funnels for implanting cells. Michail has been working for Bath Iron Works since 1987. His wife is a trained electronic technician who is currently employed by Chapman Electric.

When Michail moved to Richmond he had no intention of becoming involved in the affairs of its Russian-speaking community. Getting a job, raising a family, and rebuilding the house were the priorities and would, he felt, leave little time for any outside activities. Moreover, except for a brief period in South River, New Jersey, he had not lived among Russian-speakers since infancy.

Nor did Michail, by then a thoroughly assimilated Russian-American, feel any strong urge to maintain Belorussian cultural traditions or pass them along to his children, none of whom speaks Russian. And, perhaps because he spent his formative years in Brazil, where the fifty-mile journey to the nearest Orthodox church limited the family's attendance to major holidays, the Church has played only a minor role in the lives of his own family. His older sister, Tassie, who married a Russian, has been keeper of the old traditions. "She taught her kids to speak Russian. Sometimes she will phone to 'remind' me of a certain Saint's day. She's asked me to join the Church here. But I told her, 'When there's *one* Orthodox church in Richmond, I'll go. But *three*? No. This is too small a town for three Orthodox churches.' Our own family *does* attend Christmas and Easter services at St. Alexander Nevsky. And we always celebrate two Christmases and two Easters—one by the Orthodox calendar, one by the Gregorian.

"No, I don't really keep up with developments in Belarus, either. Occasionally someone hands me a news article about it, but I no longer read or write Russian, even though I still speak it fluently. I'd like to visit there some day. The family has relatives still living in the same village. My brother-in-law went back. Says nothing's changed

. . . unpaved streets, little picket fences, chickens and pigs running around, no electricity. So we've *talked* about going for a visit, maybe buying a little land there."

In short, Michail had clearly distanced himself from ethnic concerns and his ethnic identity long before coming to Richmond. In spite of that, and in spite of the energies required by his work, his family, and the house, he soon found himself deeply and personally involved in the affairs of Richmond's Russian-speaking settlement—especially of its older residents.

"Well, I got to know some of the Russians here. And I felt they were too quiet, unwilling to stand up for their own interests. And the town's selectmen at that time I felt were kind of ignoring us," he says, meaning the Russian-speaking residents. "They didn't show enough awareness that we all worked hard, paid our taxes. And if the town told them to do something, they *jumped.* I remember once the town changed the landscaping of a road, causing run-off to drain right into some of the Russians' basements. They mentioned it to town officials, but got the run-around. So they came to me to get it sorted out . . . it was a case of doing things to their properties without their permission. I tried to get the old-timers to be more active, but they were always afraid of officials, afraid to say 'no' to town requests."

So Michail, who—unlike the great majority of Richmond's Russian-speakers—had acquired a fair understanding of how local U.S. politics worked and how to maneuver effectively within the system—decided to take a direct part in it. "At first I served on the Board of Zoning Appeals. But I soon found out that to get anything done you had to be on the Board of Selectmen. So I ran for selectman—only the second Russian to do that since they began arriving here in 1950—and got elected."

It is clear that Michail felt his unique contribution as a selectman was to represent the older Russian-speaking settlers' interests and concerns—something many were unable or unwilling to do themselves. "You wouldn't believe how reluctant they were to deal with authority—*any* authority. Take a simple thing like a bill. If they got one of any sort, they'd pay it without raising any question, even if they thought it might be incorrect. It's not so true now. But earlier I'd tell them, 'Come to town meetings. And raise your hand. Nothing will happen to you.' They'd say, 'Oh, that's okay for *you*, because it's *you*.' 'No, no,' I'd tell them. '*You* can do it, too.' I also tried to assure them that they should shop outside of town if prices were lower there . . . 'No one will try to get even with you for doing that.' But they were skeptical about that.

"They also balked at applying for state money to repair their homes—money that was set aside for low-income people, which they certainly were. The loans were at one percent interest; but if they stayed in the home for five years, it did not have to be repaid. But the Russians could not *believe* that the government would give them money . . . there had to be a catch to it." Then there was the matter of pride. "It took me *years*," says Michail, "to convince one elderly Russian friend to apply for food stamps. When she finally did, she said, 'All right; but don't tell anybody.' Even though she was entitled to them, she was embarrassed about accepting them."

In fact much of Michail's work in behalf of the Russian settlers involved just such personal intervention with governmental authorities. "In the big flood of 1987—one of the Kennebec's 'Hundred-Year Floods'—only one Richmond home was flooded. It belonged to this old Russian lady. Her cats woke her up in the middle of the night, and there was six feet of water on the first floor. She almost drowned. But no town officials went to see her house afterward—not one. It took me three months of paperwork, plus assistance from the Church and private citizens, to get federal and state aid to restore her house—$30,000—which she didn't have to repay.

"Then, even after she got the money, she cleaned the mud off all her old dishes. And she didn't want to close up her well, which was contaminated. So I told the town guys, 'Just close it and hook her up to town water.' Then I found out she wasn't using her new washing machine. 'Why not?' 'Well, there's no place for the water to go out,' she says. In her old machine she could see the wringer pipe. In the new one she didn't see any pipe, and was afraid the water would flood the kitchen. So she went on washing by hand."

What about mutual help among the Russian settlers? "There hasn't been much of that," Michail feels. "At least there haven't been any formal arrangements . . . no pension funds or anything like that. The old people here did not trust anyone enough to manage such a fund. Many of them wouldn't even put their own money into a checking account. But the churches would help out their own parishioners, of course. And Russian families living near each other will tend to keep an eye on one another. They'll phone if they think someone's in trouble. We have three Russian-speaking homes in our neighborhood. And even where they come from different ethnic backgrounds and don't get together socially, they will help each other . . . pick up groceries if a neighbor is sick, that sort of thing."

Gradually more and more of the settlers learned to look after their own interests in the new and strange environment of local U.S. politics, and to trust and feel comfortable with local institutions and non-Russian officials. Moreover, in the last few years, those elderly Russian-speakers most in need of help, either through physical disability or language difficulties, have for the most part either died or moved away. So there is no longer a need for fellow-Russians to represent them on local boards and committees.

Meanwhile the two Grizkewitsch daughters were growing up and attending local schools. Michail began to get actively involved in local issues affecting his children. "The girls liked baseball and wanted to play on their primary school's softball team. I helped them with their applications. But the school said no, the team was boys only. I said what about a girls team? No, there was no money for that. I kept on complaining. Some other girls' parents joined me. So the school got a grant from the local Little League to buy bats and balls so we could have a girls' team."

Michail acknowledges that he has a somewhat stubborn, combative streak in pushing for what he believes is right. He clearly enjoys the rough give-and-take of local town meeting politics, and has continued to be active in school affairs, long after the Grizkewitsch children left school. As an elected member of the local school board he has played a leading role in winning grants and getting local funds to overhaul the primary school, which had badly deteriorated. "We replaced the boiler with a new one, and got the town to remove exposed asbestos from the walls and ceilings. Then we got town money to replace the school's roof beams, which sagged dangerously under the heavy snows in the winter of 1992-93. That all cost money, and divided the town . . . there were a lot of angry people,"

Michail recalls with a smile. "So if I decide to run again, I may not be reelected."

The three Grizkewitsch children are adults now. One is a computer specialist, another a nurse, and the third a policeman currently enrolled in a police academy course. All married non-Russians outside the Orthodox church. Family photographs adorn the living-room walls. Michail notes with special pride that all the children, and their spouses as well, are independent and highly competitive, hardworking people. "They all follow our family's tradition of saving money and avoiding debt. And they all stand up for what they believe is right."

PART FOUR

THE LIFE OF THE COLONY: AN OVERVIEW

Those Russians worked very hard. Never asked for credit . . . probably wouldn't have got it anyway, they had so little money. So they bought only what they could pay for. Very slowly they acquired farm animals, just one cow or horse at a time.

–Freeda Witham, 1995 interview

We visit . . . and entertain our Russian neighbors, as do many of our friends. . . . We exchange foods, flowers, and garden products, discuss world affairs, politics, local problems . . . . Their assimilation . . . was not instantaneous, but rather was earned as they lived among us and we came to know them intimately.

–Leon and Wynnefred Shepard,
Maine Sunday Telegram, June 1969

FAMILY AND WORK

TO THE RUSSIAN-SPEAKING REFUGEES who settled in Maine's Kennebec Valley after World War II, family, family loyalty, and family obligations were by far the dominant factors in their lives and behavior. In part this was a carryover of Eastern Europe's traditional extended family: the large, interdependent, multi-generational family living together in the same village.

For the refugees these traditional ties were reinforced by their own life experiences, particularly the violent dislocations they went through during World War II. Survival itself in many cases depended on the actions and mutual support of family members. After surviving the flight from battle zones and enduring the hardships of forced labor and the uncertainties of the Displaced Persons camps, family ties remained paramount. Restarting their lives in their adoptive homeland—the struggle to find jobs, housing, and financial help—found the new immigrants once again turning to family members for support. Emotionally, too, the family remained important as the only personal link to past lives in a homeland left behind forever.

In some cases where families had been separated and contact lost during the war, Maine's refugees were later able to locate lost relatives and bring them to the United States. Eugene and Alexandra Sherbakoff located her mother "living in the same Belgrade apartment where I had last seen her ten years before," as well as two married sisters, all of whom they helped resettle in America.

Many of the valley's Russian-speaking families were multi-generational. The oldest members were by then in their sixties and seventies, often in ill-health from the privations of war and forced labor. Those no longer able to work were looked after by their children. Yet some of these elderly parents lived into their nineties, by which time many required full-time care because of illness and senility. Even though family income was in many cases low enough to qualify for free or nearly free nursing-home care, by far the majority of their children refused to consider a nursing facility. As a result the child, in most cases a daughter, became virtually house-bound and could not take on or continue an outside job. Yelena Schumejko, whose mother died in 1996 at the age of ninety after a long siege of Alzheimer's, expressed the feeling common to these caregiving children: "I owe my mother so much, I just could not abandon her for strangers to take care of." In those cases where a nursing facility became the last, necessary resort, the children felt serious pangs of guilt.

Almost all the children, now middle-aged, who were contacted in the course of writing this book, spoke of being encouraged and prodded by their parents—regardless of the parents' background and class status—to get a good education as the route to economic security. Both parents and children stressed the values of hard work, avoiding debt, and living within the law. There was pride in the family's record in paying taxes due despite occasional economic setbacks, some serious.

Even within the same family, however, children showed markedly different attitudes toward retaining and passing along the parents' ethnic and cultural traditions. Many of the settlers' children born abroad during World War II and educated in the United States married Americans from non-Russian backgrounds. In some cases they have forgotten the Russian language—a loss which most now regret. Some have left the Orthodox church. Others—the women, more often than the men—have retained their faith and "old-country" language, married in the Orthodox church, and carried on the family traditions with their own children, despite having husbands who, in many cases, have different ethnic and religious roots. Indeed, even among the most ethnically lapsed of the old immigrants' children, many continue to attend Orthodox Christmas and Easter services, and to celebrate two Christmases: the Western by the Gregorian calendar, and the Russian Orthodox by the Julian calendar, a week later.

Given the rapid and total assimilation of these first generation Russian-Americans, now middle-aged, into the American mainstream, it is perhaps surprising how many *have* made the extra effort required to keep the old traditions alive in the face of the pervasiveness of the dominant American cultural influences. For some, at least, the effort reflected a belated pride in their ethnic roots. For others those roots had remained strong in spite of "growing up American."

Maintaining family ties with relatives who remained in the old country was of course especially difficult, and even dangerous, while that country was part of the Soviet Union. The Soviet government sometimes approved such links, particularly when they involved a flow of scarce U.S. dollars which the recipient had to exchange at the U.S.S.R. State Bank for rubles of limited purchasing power. But correspondence between Soviet citizens and foreigners also was used as a pretext for arresting people during the various purges and anti-Western campaigns carried out under Stalin and some of his successors. Several Richmond settlers mention receiving messages from relatives in the U.S.S.R. asking them *not* to write or send packages. "They told us it could get them into serious trouble as suspected spies," said one, "so we broke off contact with them."

Nor, until the Gorbachev regime's *glasnost* (openness) policy in 1986, was it prudent for Russian settlers here to visit their relatives in the Soviet Union. Since then a fair number of local Russian-speaking residents have gone back for short stays. Pavel Vaulin was surprised at the changes he saw, particularly the territorial expansion of Siberian cities like Yekaterinburg, since he left Siberia in 1941. In 1992, however, when Maria Sachno revisited the small, remote village in Ukraine which she had last seen fifty years before, she found almost nothing changed. "Roads were unpaved, and deep in mud. The houses were just the same, still primitive . . . no indoor plumbing at all. And food was so scarce . . . a loaf of bread costs my sister a half-week's pension." None of the Kennebec Valley's Russian-speaking residents—even those who were the most curious to see the former homeland—have so far shown any intention of returning there to live.

*   *   *   *   *

For most of the settlers, finding work in the valley was of paramount importance. Few had arrived in the U.S. with any money. Even those who had come earlier and found jobs in the industrial cities of New Jersey and elsewhere had, by the time they decided to come to Maine, in most cases saved only a few thousand dollars: just about enough to buy a run-down farm or village house.

Finding jobs in the depressed towns along the Kennebec, however, was difficult—even for Maine natives, many of whom had been forced to seek work outside the area in the early postwar years. How much more difficult, then, for the new settlers with little or no fluency in English, or whose education had stopped during the war years. Like most immigrants, many of the Russian-speaking newcomers found that the language barrier forced them to accept jobs that were lower-paying and less prestigious than those they had held before. Eugene Sherbakoff, a famous actor and director in prewar Belgrade's Russian theater, worked as a part-time cook. His wife Alexandra, a well-known professional actress and singer there, found a job at a Richmond factory sewing uppers on shoes, and "was glad to have the job." Wasyl Krochmaluk had edited a newspaper in the Ukrainian capital of Kiev until his arrest and imprisonment by Soviet authorities in the 1930s. After escaping, he became a leader in the Ukrainian underground. Shortly after emigrating to the United States in the early 1960s, Krochmaluk and his wife, who had been trained as a nurse, bought a 120-acre farm in the valley. There these two educated, city-bred immigrants raised cows and goats to pay off the loan on the farm.

Like Alexandra Sherbakoff, however, many of the new immigrants with limited English felt fortunate to get jobs in local factories. At the Clarostat factory, located in the center of Richmond, Russian-speaking employees made up roughly ten percent of its workforce of 90-100. They accounted for a much higher share of workers at the

Etonic shoe factory, the town's major employer. In the late 1950s and early 1960s the factory's stitch room, alone, employed nearly 100 women, sixty of whom were Russian-speaking. It was hard work, with daily piecework norms. But few complained. A former worker recalls her reluctance to speak out when one of the (non-Russian) foremen appeared to show favoritism in assigning bonus work: "I was afraid I would lose my job if I lodged a complaint."

Among the new immigrants, artisans and experienced farmers generally made the most rapid and successful job adaptation. A carpenter needed very little English — "I already knew how to read plans and diagrams," said one. And most Russian immigrant farmers knew how to construct simple buildings and care for livestock, thus enabling them to become largely self-sufficient. Although the colony's farmers experienced problems, their lack of fluency in English was not a severe handicap. Far more serious were the sweeping changes in marketing conditions, particularly the closure of Maine's largest chicken-processing plants in the late 1960s and early 1970s.

The next generation — those who were raised and educated in the United States — seem to have done at least as well economically as their native-born classmates. Many are college graduates, and most others are skilled technicians. Among those first children still living in the area are a university professor, a bank manager, a state educational media director, a highway planning specialist, a computer consultant, a precision machinist, and a police officer. Typical of the group's skilled technicians are Valya Kotov, who works as a draftsman at Bath Iron Works, and Andy Krochmaluk, whose varied careers include those of a self-taught professional photographer, an Army neuro-psychiatric specialist, a carpenter, and an architectural draftsman. Among several traced who now live out of the area are a psychiatric social worker, a State Department interpreter, and a U.S. Air Force officer.

While this list is no more than a sample, it suggests that the valley's Russian-speaking community has followed the longstanding assimilation pattern of other immigrants to the United States. The struggles and dreams of the original settlers have yielded a harvest of educated and skilled mainstream Americans in their children and grandchildren.

THE CENTRAL ROLE OF THE CHURCH

EASTERN ORTHODOXY was introduced into Russia in A.D. 1015—several centuries *before* a central Russian state had come into being. During those centuries the Church grew in unity and power, fulfilling many of the day-to-day functions of a government: property rights, family disputes, medical practice, and the clergy were all subject to ecclesiastical courts. When a state was finally established in the late 1400s, the self-declared "Tsar" Ivan III announced that Russia had been chosen by God to succeed Constantinople as the center of Eastern Orthodoxy. This marked the beginning of the close and often conflicted relationship of the Russian state and its official Church.[1]

The Church continued to play a vital role in the lives of the people and the monarchy until 1922, when Stalin closed it down. Only in 1943, when he needed to bolster flagging support for the war among the exhausted and suffering Soviet people, did Stalin restore the Church. In return for a declaration of loyalty to the Soviet state, Stalin released nineteen bishops from labor camps to declare Metropolitan Sergei the Patriarch.

Meanwhile Russian Orthodoxy in the United States did not escape the acrimony and divisions of Russian émigré politics. In the 1920s Russian émigrés in America affiliated with the global Russian Orthodox Church Abroad, cutting all ties with Moscow. When most of that body chose to reestablish a link to the Moscow Patriarch in 1946, the American church and others split off to establish the Russian Orthodox Church Outside Russia with its own Patriarch in Canada. In 1988 this church had 150,000 U.S. members in 135 parishes, including St. Alexander Nevsky Church in Richmond.[2]

Founded by *Corpus* members and consecrated in 1953, St. Alexander Nevsky was originally a chapel housed in the *Corpus* veterans' home—the old Southard mansion next door to the present church. It thus began life close to the old Tsarist veterans and their families: even its name was that of a thirteenth-century warrior-saint. One of its early priests, Father Afanasi Donetskoy, had been an officer in the Tsar's Cossack army.

The church quickly became the center of the colony's cultural and social life. Saints' days were the occasion of many observances. In July 1958 a memorial service to mark the fortieth anniversary of the Tsar's death drew more than a hundred people. As described in the local press, "Flags of all the Cossacks decorated the church and the Russian Imperial flag held the place of honor."[3]

Every year on October fifteenth, St. Alexander Nevsky services celebrate the *pokrová*—an event in the dawn of Cossack history when the Virgin is said to have placed a "cloak of fog" over a besieged Cossack force, enabling it to escape a Muslim army.

The church conducted religious instruction and Russian language classes for parish children, and organized Christmas pageants at which the children performed traditional dances and plays based on Russian fairy tales. Parish members also arranged help for elderly and ill members, and held annual bake sales of Russian delicacies to celebrate Richmond Days. Most important, the combination of Orthodox faith and practice were the greatest single force binding the settlers together. The church was the one institution linking them *all* emotionally and spiritually. Whether they left Russia with the First Wave or the Second, whether they were Ukrainian, Great Russian, or Belorussian, from village or city, all shared the same 900-year-old faith and a liturgy that had changed little over the centuries. Once inside the church, parishioners felt immediately at home. Icons flickering in soft candle light, the a capella choir singing in old church Slavonic, the familiar liturgy, the choral dialogue between priest and choir, the air heavy with incense: all this created a warm, nurturing homeland of the spirit.

Yet, as with any religious group anywhere, the local Russian Orthodox community has not been immune to dissension. Strong personal feelings on all aspects of church affairs were likely to be especially intense among the many parishioners for whom the local church was the only organization in which they continued to play an active role.

Only on one or two occasions, however, has really serious dissension occurred—serious enough in one instance in the 1960s to split the St. Alexander Nevsky congregation and lead a dissident minority to establish a separate church a few blocks away. Members of both churches are reluctant to talk about the split. They stress that it did not reflect any differences over religion or religious practices. The underlying cause appears to have been a growing resentment over the militancy of St. Alexander Nevsky's lay leadership, dominated at that time by *Corpus* members. As "old émigrés" who had fought under the last Tsar, they openly advocated restoration of the monarchy and celebrated the glory of the Russian Empire. That attitude rankled some of the Ukrainians and others in the parish who saw the Empire as neither democratic nor benign, especially in its treatment of ethnic minorities.

This resentment eventually surfaced in a dispute over church funds. The *Corpus* officer responsible for keeping the church's financial records allegedly balked at providing the detailed accounting demanded by some of the parishioners.

The dissidents, mostly Ukrainian and Cossack families, left St. Alexander Nevsky and established St. Nicholas Orthodox Church. When the diocese seemed unwilling to assign a priest to a second church in the same village, the St. Nicholas congregation affiliated with a different Orthodox group in 1970: the Russian Orthodox Church in America. This group recognized the Moscow Patriarch as its head, but enjoyed autonomous status. It was also much smaller than the main Orthodox church: fewer than 10,000 members and thirty-eight parishes throughout the United States.

Sadly, the new St. Nicholas Orthodox Church itself experienced a split a few years later which led some members to leave and join the even smaller Ukrainian Autocephalic Church of the Holy Cross Elevation. This split, like the other, followed a dispute over the handling of church funds.

The most publicized dispute occurred in 1976. It, too, had nothing to do with religion. The issue was a legal one: who owns the St. Alexander Nevsky Church and the land on which it stands? Formerly a barn, the church had been built on land next door to the Southard mansion. Both land and buildings were owned by a foundation run by the *Corpus*. When the church was constructed, however, contributions of cash, skilled labor, icons, and church furnishings had been donated by the *entire parish*, not only its *Corpus* members. There was an oral understanding that the church and the land it occupies would in due course become the property of the parish.

The ownership issue faded from attention for sixteen years until 1976, when the foundation (i.e., the *Corpus*) decided to sell the Southard mansion, along with the church building and land. The ownership should, of course, have been set down in legally binding deeds at the time church construction began. It seems likely, however, because of the close and overlapping membership of church and *Corpus* at the time, that no one even considered that such an issue would ever arise. Hence there seemed little reason to call in outside lawyers to formalize their understanding. The 1976 dispute was very quickly settled, conveying ownership to the parish. In 1996 the church finally received a formal deed to the church and the land on which it stands.

St. Alexander Nevsky Church survived these and other, less-serious crises. As of early 1997 it remained the largest, best-attended of Richmond's Orthodox places of worship. Alone of the three, it has a full-time priest and holds regular services three days a week, plus others to observe special Orthodox holy days. Father Chad Williams, the priest since 1987, has attracted some younger, mostly non-Russian-speaking families to the parish to help fill out the thinning ranks of older, long-standing members. A handful of the latter still remain loyal and active parishioners, however. For the benefit of the newer parishioners, Saturday services are conducted in English—a change that saddens the stalwart oldsters who remember the glory days of the 1960s, when new arrivals in the colony swelled the numbers of Russian-speaking worshippers. At the town's July celebration of Richmond Days in 1995, however, young and old Russian voices still floated across the churchyard, while a *samovar* hissed and parish women set out an array of homemade *pirozhki* and other Russian delicacies, which by now have become an acquired taste among many townsfolk.

Probably ninety percent of the Kennebec Valley's Russian-speaking settlers were Orthodox Christians who might not have come had there been no Orthodox church in the community. Yet a small group of Russian Baptist families also settled there in the late 1950s. Day

Kokarev, an ordained minister and deacon of the Russian Baptist Church in South River, New Jersey retired to Richmond in 1959 and opened a church in the Captain Carney house, now a funeral home, across Church Street from St. Alexander Nevsky.

"We had been spending summers in Dresden for some years before that," recalls Day Kokarev Jr., a psychiatric social worker living in Montpelier, Vermont. "But my father believed his mission was to transmit the faith, preach the Gospel. As soon as he retired he took up the notion of planting a church in the Russian community.

"His conversion had come in the wake of a traumatic event in the First World War, when he was a soldier in the Tsar's army. A building where he was quartered received a direct shell hit, and he was the sole survivor. Not exactly a 'battlefield conversion,' but from my work as a psychotherapist I know that, in the face of an overwhelming event—what used to be called 'shell-shock'—a person's world—and life-view can be forever changed. My father's *visible* scars were Parkinson-like tremors which began after that event and continued all his life."

After emigrating to the United States in 1920, Day Kokarev Sr. settled in New Jersey, studied at the International Baptist Seminar, and worked as a carpenter and contractor. He remained active in the affairs of the Russian-Ukrainian Baptist Union, founded in 1901.

"My father's church in Richmond opened its doors in 1959 with around twenty members. A few months later, however, he suffered a massive stroke, which virtually paralyzed him. I remember staying with him one Sunday when he was ill . . . he could hear the hymn-singing downstairs, and cried as he listened. He died within six months at the age of sixty-six.

"I admire what he was able to do with his life. I doubt that I could have done the same in his circumstances. He's been gone for more than thirty-five years; but of course we always carry the parent inside us." A man named Ivan Swatco succeeded him in Richmond, but the church only lasted a short time after that.

SOCIAL, CULTURAL, AND POLITICAL ACTIVITIES

SOCIAL LIFE IN THE SETTLEMENT, particularly during the early years, revolved around families, as well as close friends from the old homeland. Indeed many of the settlers had come to the area on the recommendation of family members or friends who had already moved there. Aside from celebrations on major holidays, social gatherings were usually small and informal: a day of picnicking and swimming at the beach, a long evening of eating, drinking, conversation, and folk songs around a table laden with familiar "old country" dishes. For larger families such events were frequently multi-generational and more inclusive: a backyard cookout at which the children and invited school friends played games, while the men tended braziers, women set out the food, and friends and neighbors socialized.

Many of the older settlers, however, had little or no social life outside the church. Some were too frail or too poor. Others, especially older couples living by themselves in the countryside, were too isolated.

Suspicions—deep-seated and often beyond reason—dampened the colonists' openness to making new friends, particularly among fellow-Russians. One Soviet defector (not a local resident) wrote of American friends wanting to introduce her to other Russians: "I could not explain that a Russian émigré community, heavily infiltrated by the K.G.B. [state security], was the last place I wanted to be."[4] She finally decided to hide her Russian ethnicity and try to pass as Portuguese.

Although the Kennebec Valley's colony was smaller and far more socially integrated than the typical Russian émigré enclave, its settlers lived with similar fears and constraints. The more activist members of the colony complained of the near-impossibility of persuading many of the settlers to join any activity involving people they did not already know and trust. Several people agreed to be interviewed for this book only on condition of anonymity, expressing fears that their stories might somehow bring harm to their adult American-born children. One local Russian, a well-spoken drifter remembered only as Svistoon—the Whistler—was suspected by some of being a

K.G.B. agent because he wandered about the town whistling and taking odd jobs, and declined to talk about his past. As an extreme example of the paranoia that could flourish in such an environment, some settlers suspected a fellow-Russian, who was a ham-radio enthusiast, of using his transmitting antenna to send messages to the K.G.B. in Moscow.

Social life in the early years took on a special luster when celebrities from the old Russian Empire, or distinguished Soviet defectors, visited the colony. Some took up summer residence. Princess Vera Romanov, a former member of Russian royalty and a cousin of the last Tsar, Nicholas II, was by far the most illustrious visitor. Her father was Grand Duke Constantine, who died in 1918 after a distinguished career as one of the more progressive and gifted members of the Tsarist elite: poet, military reformer, and patron of scientific research. The Princess and her mother fled Russia in 1918 and spent the next thirty years in Britain and other West European countries. She first visited Richmond in 1954 as a guest and honorary member of the St. Alexander Nevsky Foundation. A 1958 visit marked the 100th anniversary of the Grand Duke's birth. It was celebrated with public readings from his poetry and vocal selections from Tchaikovsky's works for which the Grand Duke had written the lyrics. The singer was Alexandra Sherbakoff.

An anonymous former member of the nobility later bought the Princess a simple house in Richmond which she used as a summer residence. A local non-Russian woman, the late Paula Umberhind, recalled visiting her there as a child. "She seemed very exotic to me. There were tapestries on the walls, and some over the windows. It was midday, but candles provided the light. She was quite regal in appearance . . . wore a Spanish comb in her hair, which was dark then. And she wore scarves. It was like an audience: she sat in a big chair, which was draped and set on a raised platform, like a throne. She was friendly, and talked about New York City and her life there."

After arriving in the United States in 1951 Princess Vera worked for the Tolstoy Foundation in New York, helping refugees from the U.S.S.R. Later she worked for the Russian Children's Welfare Society, which provided aid to Russian children behind the Iron Curtain. Vera Patkovsky, a friend of hers in Richmond, recalls that the Princess was poor, yet was frequently asked and expected to be patroness to various Russian émigré causes. "My Lady *had* kept a few jewels: a ring and bracelet given her by the Tsar's mother. And a string of really valuable pearls. She gave one pearl each year as a birthday present to her nephew's daughter."

Lydia Rennenkampf, another celebrity associated with the old regime, was the daughter of a famous general who had led a major Russian offensive in World War I. She had made her own mark as a front-line nurse with the Tsar's armies and later with Denikin's White Russian force in the civil war. After moving to Richmond in 1958, Ms. Rennenkampf served as secretary to the *Corpus* veterans' group. Both the *Corpus* and the local Russian drama troupe frequently called on her as an interpreter at various events to which non-Russians were invited.

Nicholas Rybakoff, once a Colonel in the Tsar's army, and his wife, the former Princess Kropotkin, were regular summer visitors. In 1932 he had begun publishing a major Russian-language daily, *Rossiya*, in New York. Later he published an English-language counterpart as well. His wife's family had been closely associated with the Romanov dynasty for many years. Both Rybakoffs became active in anti-Soviet causes in this country.

Count Ivan Tolstoy bought a house on Richmond's Pleasant Street. Grandson of the world-famous writer, the Count served as choirmaster in St. Alexander Nevsky Church for many years before retiring to another Russian Orthodox community in Jordanville, New York.

The artist Nikodin Belenkov and his wife settled in Richmond in 1957. Belenkov and his wife were interned in a German labor camp during World War II, and came to the United States through the efforts of the Tolstoy Foundation. A graduate of the prestigious Moscow Art School, Belenkov taught art in Cleveland before coming to Maine, where he became well-known for his exquisite oil paintings, including nostalgic country scenes of old Russia—*troikas* dashing through a snowy landscape, peasant cottages among birch trees. He is best-known, however, for the large, elaborate icons representing major Orthodox saints, painted on the interior walls of St. Alexander Nevsky Church. He also painted many scenes of rural Richmond and the Kennebec River. He died in Richmond in 1970.

The most famous Second Wave émigré to visit the area is Alexander Solzhenitsyn. The dissident writer, whose *Gulag Archipelago* gave the world its most vivid picture of life in Soviet prison camps, made his home in Vermont, but had friends among the Kennebec Valley's Russian settlers.

As the colony's numbers swelled in the late 1950s, social activities expanded into larger and more public functions. Some were openly political. In May 1958 the local *Corpus* veterans, together with members of the area's Don Cossack organization, jointly sponsored an "Anti-Communist meeting on Free Russia in the Free World." Speakers included Bishop Nikon, head of the Russian Orthodox Church Outside Russia, and Col. Anatoli Rogozhin, national head of the *Corpus*, among others. Although open to the public, the program was conducted entirely in Russian, suggesting that its message was directed chiefly at America's Russian-speaking émigrés. Similar, though larger, meetings were held in 1959 and 1961.

In July 1958 a local Russian cast, many of whom had been professional artists in pre-World War II Europe, presented the first of the colony's theatrical performances: two one-act comedies by Chekhov. They were directed by Eugene Sherbakoff, who had directed professional Russian theater companies in prewar Europe. The performance was in Russian, with English narration by Maria Dobrynin, a retired Russian actress. The program included Russian folk melodies sung by Alexandra Sherbakoff.

In May 1959 the troupe presented Chekhov's comedy, *The Anniversary*, at a local hall, to raise funds for a local Russian library. They were joined by local Russian children in a dance performance of an ancient Russian fairy tale, *The Golden Lake*.

Sherbakoff's group went on to perform Gogol's *Inspector-General* at Bowdoin and Colby colleges, the Augusta Players theater, and for other mostly non-Russian audiences. Lydia Rennenkampf gave a synopsis of the play in English before each performance. Sherbakoff himself served as consultant for the Bowdoin Masque and Gown's 1964 production of the Gogol comedy in English.

The colony also spawned two ethnic-based cultural organizations. The Association of Ukrainian-Americans in New England was founded in 1964 by Wasyl Krochmaluk, a former newspaper editor in the

Ukraine. Although the association's activities and membership have fluctuated over the years, at one time its members numbered over 150, forty of whom came from the Richmond area. The local group organized parties and picnics where Ukrainian families came together to enjoy native food, music, and dancing. On a rainy October Saturday in 1994, more than forty people, including several young Ukrainian defectors and their Ukrainian-born wives, attended the association's fall picnic in Richmond's Grange Hall. The leaders of the local branch also have promoted interest in Ukrainian culture, and supported Ukrainian independence (and Ukrainian defectors) prior to 1991 when that region formed part of the former Soviet Union.

In 1972 settlers organized the Slavophile Society. Named after a nineteenth-century Russian movement, the society had both social and cultural goals, including promoting Slavic literature, acquiring land for a headquarters and retirement complex, and organizing dances and other events. Its activity gradually faded over the years, however, and plans for a building fell victim to financial stringency and declining interest. The society is now defunct.

By the 1990s most of the First Wave émigrés—the settlers who had been the most active in *Corpus*, Cossack, and Orthodox Church organizations—had either died, moved away, or for other reasons were no longer actively involved in such organizations. The next generation—people now in their seventies—are largely assimilated and have therefore been far less interested in ethnic-based activities, other than the Church. Their children are now in their forties and fifties and totally assimilated into the United States mainstream. Except for the handful of Ukrainian-American nationalists already mentioned, these middle-aged children have no interest in perpetuating or reviving the local ethnic organizations that were so important to the early settlers forty years ago.

INTERFACE WITH THE LOCAL COMMUNITY

IN THE EARLY 1950S America's postwar boom in jobs, housing, and construction was bypassing the Kennebec Valley. Many young people were leaving, or had already left, to seek work elsewhere. The physical appearance of most valley towns had changed so little over the years that a late-returning Civil War veteran would have easily found his way home along the streets and town centers he had known ninety years earlier. The rapid influx of several hundred Russian-speaking immigrant families into this quiet, seemingly changeless valley could hardly have gone unnoticed. The initial reaction was one of mild, Yankee-type curiosity. Who *were* these strange people speaking a strange language? Like the local Mainers, the early Russian-speaking settlers kept largely to themselves. Finding jobs, and restoring and improving the mostly run-down old houses and farms they had bought for a few thousand dollars, left them little time to invest in seeking friends among their non-Russian neighbors. But they did begin appearing as shoppers in local grocery, hardware, and feed-and-grain stores. And local people noticed their sometimes strange ways. Some of the older townsfolk laughingly recall waiting in line at the meat counter while an elderly Russian farmer tried to bargain over the price of beef. Gerald Brown, a former Richmond selectman, remembers seeing Russians "walking down the middle of the street rather than using the sidewalks."

The Russians were quickly and mainly noted, however, for their thrift and hard work. Retired journalist Freeda Witham, a life-long valley resident now in her eighties, remembers their early struggles: "Those Russians worked very hard. Never asked for credit . . . probably wouldn't have got it anyway, they had so little money. So they bought only what they could pay for. Very slowly they acquired farm animals, just one cow or horse at a time. My brother-in-law sold feed and grain. He told of two Russians who bought an old, dilapidated place near the Richmond dump. The first year they planted a big garden and dug the whole thing up by hand, with spades. One of them came to his store to buy beans, which came in great, heavy sacks—*one* was more than my brother-in-law cared to lift—and this Russian fellow threw two bags across his back and took off as though they were nothing at all!"

Both the "Russians" and the "Americans"—the terms used by each local group to describe the other in the early years—agree that little mingling occurred between them then. No Welcome Wagon or specially organized "get acquainted" events were organized for the new settlers. It simply did not appear to be rural Maine's way. Nor did Slavic names appear on the rosters of the Grange, I.O.O.F., or other traditional American organizations.

Not surprisingly, the first friendly contacts took place between neighbors. Lloyd Ferris, a journalist with the *Portland Press Herald*, remembers a surprise knock at the door one midwinter evening:

"My wife and I at that time, the early 1960s, were trying to live self-sufficiently on our two-acre farm. And our Russian neighbor, John Supruniuk, who was a chicken-farmer, had watched our efforts and saw we were having a hard time. So one night around Christmas . . . there was snow all around . . . he knocked on the door and handed me a bag with six live chickens inside it. 'Here. You take. Chop heads and eat.' It was the first time I'd ever killed a chicken! The Supruniuks remain good friends. And we keep in touch with their children, too."

Friendly gestures were also made in the other direction. One winter when her family's farm was failing, local delivery men brought Yelena Schumejko the only Christmas toys she was to receive that year (see page 113). The settlers did, however, encounter some hostility and suspicion among local people. The 1950s saw the heating-up of the Cold War and its accompanying rhetoric. Anti-Soviet feelings occasionally spilled over to anything "Russian," including the area's virulently anti-Soviet immigrants, most of whom had, themselves, been victims of the Soviets in one way or another. Local incidents were few and isolated, however: young schoolboys throwing stones at "Commies'" (i.e., Russians') houses, for example. Larry Chadwick Jr. of Dresden recalls overhearing a serious discussion among men at a local store over a rumor that the colony's White Russian founder, Baron von Poushental, was secretly testing a submarine in a nearby lake.

A few longtime local residents expressed mild annoyance at the press for "all the publicity the Russians here have been getting . . . you'd think nothing else mattered here," one said. In fact the colony did *not* receive much press coverage. The main reporting over several decades was given to the annual Orthodox celebrations of Christmas and Easter, which gave rise to Sunday feature articles with large photos of the churches and services, as well as Russian and

Ukrainian holiday recipes and personal descriptions of Easter egg traditions. On a couple of occasions when reporters wrote what were considered unfriendly pieces about the colony, Mainers and settlers alike took them to task. In May 1968 Anna Tuniks wrote a letter to the *Kennebec Journal* saying a local reporter's story on the settlement "had too much sadness," and rejecting his analogy to elephants coming together to die:

> We came here to live and build. Some of us lost hundreds of acres of land, estates, and mansions [in the Revolution]. In Europe we toiled, saved, built and lost again. Now, [in the 1950s] we considered ourselves fortunate to become part of this country. This time we were ready to build again, true . . . on a smaller scale, with less strength and with a quaint accent in English . . . [the cemetery may be waiting for us] but that does not stop us from living life, tending our gardens and wanting to be useful. [Thus] we are . . . happy that we could take [local college students] into our homes . . . teach them our language and share our rich culture with them.[5]

In June 1969, Leon and Wynnefred Shepard took issue with a piece in the *Maine Sunday Telegram* in which the reporter wrote that there was "little assimilation of the Russian newcomers" into the local community:

> We visit . . . and entertain our Russian neighbors, as do many of our friends, and they reciprocate. We exchange foods, flowers, and garden products, discuss world affairs, politics, local problems and friends' illnesses and problems. . . . Their assimilation into the community was not instantaneous, but rather was earned as they lived among us and we came to know them intimately. We consider the several mixed marriages evidence of pretty close relationships, and we witness several more budding romances. How much closer can one get?"[6]

By the late 1950s the local schools had become an important vehicle of assimilation as more and more Russian children were enrolled.

In 1955 Nikita Gursky and Steven Gurin appeared as the King and Simple Simon in Richmond Elementary School's performance of an operetta, *The Birthday Pie*. Alexander Podressoff, who gave the graduation talk (on science) at Emerson Grammar School in 1959, was elected to the National Honor Society at Richmond High School three years later. Some Russian parents also became involved: during National Hot Lunch Week Lydia Kovtuschenko, whose two sons attended Marcia Buker School, provided the recipes on the day set aside for Russian specialties.

In 1967 local school officials organized and trained volunteers to conduct English language classes for elderly Russian residents—a program that continued for several years. The students, some in their eighties, signed up mainly to be able to pass the U.S. citizenship exam. Genesee Hickson later recalled her experience as a volunteer instructor:

"They *really* wanted to learn. Mostly basic, practical stuff: how to order stamps at the Post Office, for example. They tried hard, hanging on our every word. Most of them passed the exam the first time. And they were so respectful . . . they'd stand whenever I entered the room, and I could never put my coat on without their help. One of them gave me a decanter of blackberry wine, not realizing that my husband and I don't drink. It played 'How Dry I Am.' We still have the decanter—*and* the wine."

A new step in the colony's outreach to Maine's non-Russian community was taken in January 1968, when six Colby College students spent the month as guests of first generation Russian-speaking families in Richmond as a special credits project. Two years later the University of Maine arranged an intensive Russian language summer program in Richmond for college and high school students. Russian families hosted the students for the seven-week course, which included folk-singing and ethnic dances as well as daily immersion in Russian language and culture. Professor Jane Knox of the Bowdoin College Russian Studies Department won a grant from the Maine Humanities Council to organize a month-long series of events in June 1981 to acquaint Maine's people with the area's Russian-speaking community. Lectures, a Slavic bazaar, and Russian folk-music performances were held in the area's five largest towns: Augusta,

Bath, Brunswick, Richmond, and Gardiner. They were followed by a week of special lectures and workshops on Russian art, literature, and music. A local *balalaika* orchestra closed the program.

Members of the Russian-speaking colony first began to take an active part in local civic affairs in the early 1970s. The late Galina Panko was elected in 1975 to Richmond's Board of Selectmen, where she initiated a successful drive to establish a town health center. She ran for office, she said later, because she wanted to help the community, particularly the aging Russian residents, who needed a local place to get medical care.[7] Reelected several times, Panko served a total of ten years and, at age seventy-eight, received Richmond's Outstanding Senior Citizen award. Basilio Lepuschenko served on Richmond's Planning Board for three years, and Michail Grizkewitsch served as a selectman and more recently as a member of the School Board.

Nor have the Russian-speaking émigrés ignored national and state politics. Richmond resident Alex Poliakoff recalls that his father made an unsuccessful run as a Democrat for the Maine legislature in the early 1970s. "He was far from being a party-liner," Alex recalls, "but he *was* seriously concerned about social issues. And he hated Richard Nixon." In 1980 George Ochrimenko, another politically active settler, organized a gathering of fellow-immigrants to meet U.S. Congressman David Emery, who was up for reelection.

EPILOGUE

THUS PASSED THE LIFE OF THE COLONY from its begin-
nings in the early 1950s through its most vital decades in the 1960s
and 70s to its fading years in the 1980s and 90s—a run of more than
forty years. Not bad for a settlement so unlikely to have taken root at
all in an economic and social environment so harsh to new trans-
plants and so far from established Russian immigrant centers. The
colonists were a mixed group, many of them elderly, none of them
wealthy, and only a few of them fluent in English when they arrived.
In the old country some had been aristocrats, some artists and pro-
fessionals, some peasants.

Life in the settlement changed gradually but markedly during
those forty-odd years. The changes mainly reflected differences in
life experiences and outlook between generations. The "Old Émigrés"—those who fled Russia during the 1917 Bolshevik revolution
and the civil war that followed—were already old by the time they
reached their Kennebec Valley sanctuary, "our last stop," as one
elderly settler dryly put it. A few of these people had lived elsewhere
in the United States since the 1920s, and had already become
Americanized. But the core group of Richmond's early settlers were
the families of *Corpus* and Cossack veterans: Tsarist soldiers who had
fled together to live in Russian enclaves in Yugoslavia after the collapse of the Russian Empire, only to be recruited again to serve
under German orders in World War II. In their final immigration, to
America, they sought not only peace and security, but solace and

comfort among their former comrades-in-arms—people who had been through the same life experiences and fought in many of the same engagements. Their strongest impressions were of *past* events, their strongest ties were to those who shared that past. Their social gatherings, and especially their anti-Communist meetings, were a continuation of their fight against the old enemy—a way to vindicate their lives, which had been molded and fired in that struggle.

Almost all of the settlement's Second Wave, those who left Russia *after* it had fallen under Soviet rule, had fled during the chaos of World War II. Though some were elderly, many were in their thirties and forties, eager to find work and raise children (and, in many cases, care for aged parents). The Russia that this Second Wave had known was a far different reality than the beloved homeland remembered and mourned by the Old Émigré group. Hence their focus was on the present and future in America. They had no interest in the old Empire and no time to listen to the war stories of their fathers and other oldsters.

As the Old Émigrés passed on, the local *Corpus*, the Cossack *stanitsa*, and the anti-Soviet meetings passed on with them, along with celebrations of Tsarist-era anniversaries. Except for a small group of Ukrainian-American nationalists, activists among the Second Wave became involved in local civic affairs, rather than ethnic-based activities.

As the First and Second Waves have faded, so, too, has the settlement's organizing vigor and strong sense of ethnic and cultural identity. By the 1970s a new generation, the Russian-Americans, most of them educated in the United States and many of them born here as well, were coming of age, entering the labor force, and starting families of their own. They have been assimilated into the broad American mainstream and, with few exceptions, are more skilled and better-educated than their parents. Most married outside their ethnic group and many, particularly the men, outside the Orthodox faith. While many have moved away, mainly to find jobs, others have remained in the area. Not surprisingly, most members of this new generation have shown little or no interest in maintaining more than token links with their ethnic and cultural past.

The valley's Russian-Americans today are far different from the inward-looking, mutually dependent group of immigrants who first arrived. The shared "old country" language and deep faith of parents and grandparents, their shared sense of a lost homeland (although visions of that homeland differed), and the accompanying feeling of uprootedness: for the new generation all this is not a shared experience, but part of family history.

From an historical perspective, the settlement has simply followed the normal evolutionary path of most immigrant communities in the United States for the last 150 years: from ethnic enclave to American mainstream in two generations, with only a few symbolic markers retained to recall the path taken.

ACKNOWLEDGMENTS

MY DEEPEST THANKS go to the members of the Russian-speaking settlement who generously agreed to share their life experiences with me. Without their amazing stories, there would be no book. Through the many days of interviews with each one, often spread over several months, I have come to know them as friends; they and their stories have become a treasured part of my own life experience.

There are others without whose help the book would have been much diminished: Freeda Witham, whose interest in the arriving Russians led to a unique series of early photographs and a collection of press clippings, all of which she graciously gave to me; the late Nikolai Protopopov of Santa Rosa, California, former Secretary of the *Russkii Corpus,* who provided me with copies of *Corpus* bulletins and newsletters from its years in Maine; Larry Chadwick Jr., who shared his warm reminiscences of hunting and socializing with the late Baron von Poushental; and Day Kokarev Jr., whose reminiscences of his father and pictures of Poushental filled important gaps in the colony's history.

Several other friends deserve special mention for their encouragement and support of the book, particularly during the dry periods in its conception and writing: Kendall Merriam, who suggested key contacts and traced some old photographs; Father Chad Williams, who paved the way for interviews with several of his parishioners; Kathy Brandes, who shared her enthusiasm for the book and her impressive knowledge of the publishing business; and Jay Robbins, who engaged the support of the Richmond Historical and Cultural Society. Genesee Hixon and the late Paula Umberhind offered useful insights on the Russians' relations with local Maine people, and the Town Clerks of the Kennebec Valley patiently helped me pull down and re-shelve twenty-five years of dusty town records.

The past year of growing friendly but rigorous dialogue with Michael Alpert and Ann Robinson have made me gradually aware of my good fortune in a publisher and editor who have approached the book with both enthusiasm and perceptive questioning. Last, but by no means least, I had the strong and loving support of my wife, Shirley Kew Jaster, who cast a critical eye on early drafts and ultimately scanned the entire text for transfer to a computer disk for the publisher.

In sum, my pride in authorship glows in full recognition that many people contributed to the end-product. I take full responsibility for any errors or omissions, however.

ENDNOTES

Chapter 1

1. *Lewiston Journal*, 18 May 1968.
2. Ibid.
3. Ibid.
4. John Slattery, Helicopter International, interview by author, 1995.
5. N. De Transehe, "The Genius of George de Bothezat." *American Helicopter*, July 1957, pp. 6-11.
6. Larry Chadwick Jr., interview by author, summer 1994.
7. Freeda Witham, interview by author, fall 1993.
8. Paula Umberhind, interview by author, summer 1994.
9. Chadwick interview.
10. Maine State business archives, Maine State Library, Augusta.
11. Chadwick interview.
12. *Novoye Russkoye Slovo (The New Russian Word)*, New York.
13. IRO data from George Fischer, *Soviet Opposition to Stalin: A Case Study in World War II* Cambridge: Harvard University Press, 1952, pp. 109-115.
14. *Kennebec Journal*, 22 May 1952.
15. *Portland Sunday Telegram*, 31 October 1954.
16. *Lewiston Journal*, 18 May 1968.
17. *Kennebec Journal*, 22 May 1952.
18. Ibid., 17 August 1953.
19. *Denver Post*, 28 October 1955.
20. *Miami Herald*, 1 February 1958.
21. *Lewiston Journal*, 18 May 1968 and *Nashi Vesti* (organ of the

Russkii Corpus) #374, 1979.

22. Vera Kotov, interview by author, fall 1993.

23. Ibid.

24. Vera Patkovsky and Alexandra Sherbakoff, interview by author, summer 1994.

25. Paul Vaulin, interview by author, fall 1993.

26. Basilio Lepuschenko, interview by author, fall 1993.

27. Freeda Witham, interview by author, fall 1993.

28. *Lewiston Journal*, 18 May 1968.

Chapter 2

1. Gennadi Sisoyan letter, translated from *Soglasiye (Assent)*, newsletter of the *Russkii Corpus*, June 1992.

2. Ibid.

3. Report translated from *Nashi Vesti*, op.cit., July 1952.

4. M. Burgureyev, *Nashi Vesti*, March 1953.

5. *Kennebec Journal*, 22 May 1952.

6. *Nashi Vesti*, June 1953.

7. Ibid.

8. Ibid.

9. *Nashi Vesti*, March 1954.

10. Report to the Foundation's first annual meeting, *Nashi Vesti*, June 1953.

11. Report to the Foundation's second annual meeting. *Nashi Vesti*, March 1954.

12. Ibid.

13. *Nashi Vesti*, June 1975.

Chapter 4

1. William Korey, *Russian Anti-Semitism, Pamyat, and the Demonology of Zionism*. Chur, Switzerland: Harwood Academic Publications, 1995, p. 2.

2. Paul Vaulin, *The Legend of Kitezh*, privately published, 1979. A revised edition was published in Russia: *Skazanie o Kitezhe*. Yekaterinburg: Lad, 1994. Another book by Vaulin, *The Regiment*

of Kitezh (Alabama, Kitezh Publications, 1977) describes the activities of an American political agent during the Cold War.

Chapter 5

1. One Cossack division was allowed to fight side by side with regular German units, and soon was further rewarded with combat medals and a unit promotion to the rank and title of Cossack Cavalry Corps. See George Fischer, *Soviet Opposition to Stalin: A Case Study in World War II*. Cambridge: Harvard University Press, 1952, p. 49, and Alexander Werth, *Russia At War, 1941-1945*. New York: Dutton Publishers, 1964, pp. 576-7.
2. N. Krasnov, *Nezabivaemoye* (The Unforgotten). In Russian. New York: Rasilyev Book Store Publishers, 1956, pp. 28-30.

Chapter 6

1. *(Maine) Standard-Examiner*, 12 September 1988.
2. See, e.g., *Yankee Magazine*, February 1978; *Country Journal*, February 1978.

Part Four

1. Nicholas Zernov, *The Russians and Their Church*. Crestwood, New Jersey: St. Vladimir's Seminary Press, 1978.
2. J. Gordon Melton, *Encyclopedia of American Religions*, fifth edition. Detroit: Gale Research, 1996. p. 276.
3. *Kennebec Journal*, 15 July 1958.
4. Alexandra Costa, *Stepping Down from the Stars: A Soviet Defector's Story*. New York, G. P. Putnam's Sons, 1986. p. 208.
5. *Kennebec Journal*, 11 May 1968.
6. *Maine Sunday Telegram*, 22 June 1969.
7. *Brunswick Times-Record*, 26 August 1985.

BIBLIOGRAPHY

On the Immigrant Experience in America

Thomas J. Archdeacon, *Becoming American: An Ethnic History*. New York: Free Press, 1983.

Philip Taylor, *The Distant Magnet: European Emigration to the U.S.A.* New York: Harper and Row, 1971.

Roger Daniels, *Coming to America: A History of Immigration and Ethnicity in American Life*. New York: Harper-Collins, 1990.

Jessie Bernard, *The Sociology of Community*. Glenview, Illinois: Scott Foresman, 1973.

On Russian Immigrants, Exiles, and Refugees

Nancy Eubank, *The Russians in America*. Minneapolis: Lerner Publications, 1986.

Rita J. Simon, *New Lives: the Adjustment of Soviet Jewish Immigrants in the United States and Israel*. Lexington, Mass: Lexington Books, 1985.

Michael Marrus, *The Unwanted: European Refugees in the Twentieth Century*. London: Oxford University Press, 1985

Helen Muchnic, *Russian Writers: Notes and Essays*. New York: Random House, 1971.

Raymond Dennett, *Negotiating With the Russians*. Boston: World Peace Foundation, 1951.

Cathy Young, *Growing Up in Moscow: Memories of a Soviet Girlhood*. New York: Ticknor and Fields, 1989.

Alexandra Costa, *Stepping Down from the Stars: A Soviet Defector's Story*. New York: G. P. Putnam's Sons, 1986.

Victor Ripp, *From Moscow to Main Street: Among the Russian* Émigrés. Boston: Little, Brown and Co., 1984.

Michael Binyon, *Life in Russia*. New York: Pantheon Books, 1983.

Russians at War

W. Bruce Lincoln, *Red Victory: A History of the Russian Civil War*. New York: Simon and Schuster, 1989.

George Fischer, *Soviet Opposition to Stalin: A Case Study in World War II*. Cambridge: Harvard University Press, 1952.

Alexander Werth, *Russia At War, 1941-1945*. New York: Dutton Publishers, 1964.

N. Krasnov, *Nezabivaemoye (The Unforgotten)*. In Russian. New York: Rasilyev Book Store Publishers, 1956.

Catherine Andreyev, *Vlasov and the Russian Liberation Movement*. Cambridge (U.K.): Cambridge University Press, 1987.

Nikolai Krasnov, *Kazachaya Tragedia 1940-1945 (The Cossack Tragedy 1940-1945)*. In Russian. New York: N.A.Bykov, Publisher, 1959.

On the Russian Orthodox Church

Nicholas Zernov, *The Russians and Their Church*. Crestwood, New Jersey: St.Vladimir's Seminary Press, 1978.

J. Gordon Melton, *Encyclopedia of American Religions*. Detroit: Gale Research, Fifth Edition, 1996.

William Korey, *Russian Anti-Semitism, Pamyat, and the Demonology of Zionism*. Chur, Switzerland: Harwood Academic Publishers, 1995.

INDEX

Roman numerals refer to photographs following page 52.